# BOOKS BY RANDALL JARRELL

### POETRY

| | |
|---|---|
| *The Rage for the Lost Penny* (in *Five Young American Poets*) | *1940* |
| *Blood for a Stranger* | *1942* |
| *Little Friend, Little Friend* | *1945* |
| *Losses* | *1948* |
| *The Seven-League Crutches* | *1951* |
| *The Woman at the Washington Zoo* | *1960* |
| *The Lost World* | *1965* |
| *The Complete Poems* | *1968* |

### ESSAYS

| | |
|---|---|
| *Poetry and the Age* | *1953* |
| *A Sad Heart at the Supermarket* | *1962* |
| *The Third Book of Criticism* | in preparation |

### FICTION

| | |
|---|---|
| *Pictures from an Institution* | *1954* |

### CHILDREN'S BOOKS

| | |
|---|---|
| *The Gingerbread Rabbit* | *1964* |
| *The Bat-Poet* | *1964* |
| *The Animal Family* | *1965* |
| *Fly by Night* | in preparation |

### TRANSLATIONS

| | |
|---|---|
| *The Golden Bird and Other Fairy Tales of the Brothers Grimm* | *1962* |
| *The Rabbit Catcher and Other Fairy Tales of Ludwig Bechstein* | *1962* |
| *Faust, Part 1* | in preparation |

### ANTHOLOGIES

| | |
|---|---|
| *The Anchor Book of Stories* | *1958* |
| *The Best Short Stories of Rudyard Kipling* | *1961* |
| *The English in England (Kipling Stories)* | *1963* |
| *In the Vernacular: The English in India (Kipling Stories)* | *1963* |
| *Six Russian Short Novels* | *1963* |
| *Modern Poetry: An Anthology* | in preparation |

# *THE THREE SISTERS*

ANTON ᴾᵃᵛˡᵒᵛⁱᶜʰ CHEKHOV

*The Three Sisters*

English Translation and Notes by

RANDALL JARRELL

*The Macmillan Company*

*Collier-Macmillan Limited / London*

*PG*
*3456*
*T8*
*J3*

Library of Congress Catalog Card Number: 69-10784

First Printing

Acknowledgments are made to Little, Brown & Co. for quotations from
Chekhov's letters from *Chekhov* by Ernest J. Simmons; also to Grove
Press for quotations from David Magarshack's *Chekhov: A Life.*

The Macmillan Company
Collier-Macmillan Canada Ltd., Toronto, Ontario

Printed in the United States of America

*Grateful acknowledgment*

*is made to* Mr. Paul Schmidt *for his excellent*

*literal translation provided for the*

*final revisions of the script and to*

Mr. Peter Kudric *for many helpful*

*conversations on the work*

# THE THREE SISTERS

# CONTENTS

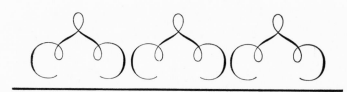

# THE
# THREE
# SISTERS

# CAST OF CHARACTERS

PROZOROV, Andrei Sergeevich

NATALYA [NATASHA] IVANOVNA, *his fiancée, then his wife*

OLGA
MASHA } *his sisters*
IRINA

KULYGIN, Fyodor Ilich, *a high school teacher, husband of*
MASHA

VERSHININ, Alexander Ignatyevich, *Lieutenant Colonel,*
*Battery Commander*

TUZENBACH, Nikolai Lvovich, *Baron, Lieutenant*

SOLYONY, Vasili Vasilevich, *Staff Captain*

CHEBUTYKIN, Ivan Romanovich, *Military Doctor*

FEDOTIK, Alexei Petrovich, *Second Lieutenant*

RODE, Vladimir Karlovich, *Second Lieutenant*

FERAPONT, *janitor from the county board, an old man*

ANFISA, *nurse, an old woman of eighty*

*The action takes place in a provincial city.*

*The Actors Studio Production in 1964*
Photograph by MARTHA HOLMES

PREMIERE PERFORMANCE JUNE 22, 1964

# THE
# MOROSCO THEATRE

The Actors Studio, Inc.

*presents*

## THE ACTORS STUDIO THEATRE

*production of*

# THE THREE SISTERS

*A Play by*
### ANTON CHEKHOV

*New English Translation by*
### RANDALL JARRELL

### THE COMPANY

| | | | |
|---|---|---|---|
| Luther Adler | Barbara Baxley | Tamara Daykarhanova | John Harkins |
| Gerald Hiken | Shirley Knight | Robert Loggia | Salem Ludwig |
| Janice Mars | Kevin McCarthy | Brooks Morton | James Olson |
| Geraldine Page | Albert Paulsen | David Paulsen | Kim Stanley |

| *Scenery Designed by* | *Costumes Designed by* | *Lighting by* |
|---|---|---|
| WILL STEVEN ARMSTRONG | THEONI V. ALDREDGE and RAY DIFFEN | FEDER |

*Directed by*
### LEE STRASBERG

# ACT I

---

THE LIVING ROOM IN THE HOUSE OF THE PROZOROVS
—*a row of columns separates it from a large dining
room at the back. Midday; outside it is sunny and bright.
In the dining room the table is being set for lunch.*
OLGA, *in the dark blue uniform of a teacher in a girls'
high school, is correcting papers, standing or walking
to and fro.* MASHA, *in a black dress, her hat on her knees,
is sitting reading a book.* IRINA, *in a white dress, stands
lost in thought.*

OLGA  Just a year ago, a year ago on this very day, Father
died—on your birthday, Irina, on the fifth of May. It was
very cold, the snow was falling. I thought I'd never live
through it; you had <u>fainted</u>, and lay there as if you were
dead. But now a year's gone by and we can remember it
calmly; you're already wearing white, your face is
radiant. . . .

[*The clock strikes twelve*]

And the clock struck just the same way then. (*A pause*)
I remember that as they took Father there the band was
playing, they fired a volley over his grave. He was a
general, he was in command of a whole brigade, and yet
there weren't many people. Of course, it was raining.

Raining hard—rain and snow.

IRINA  Why think about it?

[*Behind the columns, in the dining room,* BARON TUZENBACH, CHEBUTYKIN, *and* SOLYONY *appear*]

OLGA  It's warm today, we can have the windows wide open—and yet there still aren't any leaves on the birches. They gave Father his brigade, we left Moscow with him, eleven years ago, and I remember distinctly that in Moscow at this time, at the start of May, everything is already in bloom; it's warm, everything is bathed in sunshine. That was eleven years ago, and yet I remember it all as if we'd left it yesterday. Oh, God! When I woke up this morning I saw that everything was light, that it was spring, and I thought my heart would burst with joy. I longed so passionately to go home.

CHEBUTYKIN  The devil it is!

TUZENBACH  Of course, it's all nonsense. (MASHA, *brooding over her book, softly whistles a tune*)

OLGA  Don't *whistle*, Masha! How can you? (*A pause*) Being at school every day and then giving lessons all afternoon—it makes my head ache all the time, the thoughts I have are an old woman's thoughts already. Really and truly, these four years I've been at the high school I've felt the strength and the youth being squeezed out of me day by day, drop by drop. And just one dream grows stronger and stronger.

IRINA  To go back to Moscow! To sell the house, finish up everything here, and—off to Moscow!

OLGA  Yes! As soon as we possibly can, to Moscow!

(CHEBUTYKIN *and* TUZENBACH *laugh*)

IRINA  Brother will probably be a professor, he won't be

living here anyway. The only thing wrong is poor Masha.

OLGA  Masha's going to come and spend the whole
summer in Moscow every summer. (MASHA *softly begins
to whistle a tune*)

IRINA  Please God, it will all come out right! (SHE *looks
out of the window*) It's such a beautiful day, I don't know
why I feel so happy. This morning I remembered it's my
birthday, and all at once I felt joyful and remembered
my childhood, when Mother was still alive. And what
marvelous thrilling thoughts I had—what thoughts!

OLGA  You're radiant today—I've never seen you lovelier.
And Masha looks lovely, too. And Andrei would be
good-looking, only he's got so fat; it isn't a bit becoming.
And I've got older and so much thinner—I suppose it's
because I get so cross at the girls at school. Today now,
I'm free, I'm at home, my head doesn't ache, I feel so much
younger to myself than I did yesterday. I'm only twenty-
eight. . . . It's all good, it's all as God means it to be,
but it seems to me that if I were married and stayed home
all day it would be better. (*A pause*) I'd love my husband.

TUZENBACH  You talk such nonsense I'm sick of listening
to you. (*Coming into the living room*) I forgot to tell
you. Today you are to be visited by our new battery
commander. His name's Vershinin.

OLGA  Really? I'm delighted.

IRINA  Is he old?

TUZENBACH  No, not very. Forty or so—forty-five at the
most. He seems quite nice—and he's certainly no fool.
Only he talks a lot.

IRINA  Is he interesting?

TUZENBACH  Yes, interesting enough—only there's a wife,
a mother-in-law, and two little girls. What's more, she's

his second wife. He goes around calling on people and telling them he has a wife and two little girls. He'll tell you that. His wife isn't exactly all there: she has long braids like a girl's, talks only of lofty things, philosophizes, and regularly tries to commit suicide—to annoy her husband, evidently. If I were Vershinin I'd have left such a woman long ago, but he puts up with it and just complains.

SOLYONY (*Entering the living room with* CHEBUTYKIN) With one hand I can only lift sixty pounds, but with two hands I can lift a hundred and eighty-two—two hundred, even. From that I deduce that two men aren't twice as strong, they're three times as strong as one man . . . or even stronger. . . .

CHEBUTYKIN (*Reading a newspaper as* HE *comes in*) For falling hair: Two ounces of naphtha in half a pint of alcohol . . . dissolve and apply daily. (HE *writes it down in his notebook*) Let's make a note of it! (*To* SOLYONY) So remember what I told you, you want to cork the bottle tight and push a glass tube down through the cork. Then you take a pinch of alum, plain ordinary alum—

IRINA   Ivan Romanich, dear Ivan Romanich!

CHEBUTYKIN   What is it, my child, my treasure?

IRINA   Tell me, why is it I'm so happy today? As if I were sailing along with the wide blue sky over me and great white birds floating across it. Why is that? Why?

CHEBUTYKIN (*Kissing both her hands tenderly*)   My white bird . . .

IRINA   When I woke up this morning and got up and bathed, all at once I felt as if everything in the world were clear to me, and I understood the way one ought to live. Dear Ivan Romanich, I understand everything. A man must work, must make his bread by the sweat of his brow,

*Andrei and Natasha*
Photograph by FRIEDMAN-ABELES

it doesn't matter who he is—and it is in this alone that
he can find the purpose and meaning of his life, his happiness, his ecstasies. Oh, how good it is to be a workman
who gets up at dawn and breaks stones in the street, or a
shepherd, or a schoolteacher who teaches children, or a
locomotive engineer! My God, it's better to be an ox, it's
better to be a plain horse, and *work*, than to be a girl who
wakes up at twelve o'clock, has coffee in bed, and then
takes two hours to get dressed. . . . Oh, how awful that
is! Sometimes I—I *thirst* for work the way on a hot day
you thirst for water. And if I don't get up early and
work, give me up forever, Ivan Romanich!

CHEBUTYKIN (*Tenderly*)  I will, I will.

OLGA  Father trained us to get up at seven. Now Irina
wakes up at seven and lies there till nine at least, and
thinks about something. And she does look so serious!
(*Laughing*)

IRINA  You're so used to considering me a child that you're
surprised I should ever be serious. I am twenty!

TUZENBACH  That thirst for work—good God, how well
I understand it! I've never worked a day in my life. I
was born in Petersburg, cold, lazy Petersburg—born into
a family that never knew what work or worry meant. I
remember that when I'd get home from cadet school a
footman would pull my boots off for me, and I'd do
something idiotic and my mother would look at me in awe,
and then be surprised when everybody else didn't. I've
been sheltered from work. But they've hardly succeeded
in sheltering me forever—hardly! The time has come: a
thundercloud is hanging over us all, a great healthy storm
is gathering; it's coming, it's already almost upon us,
and is going to sweep out of our society the laziness, the

indifference, the contempt for work, the rotten boredom.
I'll work—and in another twenty-five or thirty years
everybody will work. Everybody!

CHEBUTYKIN  *I'm* not going to work.

TUZENBACH  You don't count.

SOLYONY  In another twenty-five years, thank God, you
won't be here on this earth. In two or three years either
you'll get apoplexy or I'll lose control of myself and
put a bullet through your head, my angel. (HE *takes a
little bottle of perfume from his pocket and sprinkles it
over his chest and hands*)

CHEBUTYKIN  I really never have done a thing. Since I
left the university I haven't lifted a finger, I haven't opened
a book—I just read the newspapers. (HE *takes another
newspaper out of his pocket*) Here we are. I know
from the papers that there was, say, somebody named
Dobrolyubov, but what he wrote I don't know. God only
knows. (*A knock is heard from the floor below*) Listen.
They want me downstairs, somebody's come to see me.
. . . I'm coming right away. Wait a minute. . . . (HE *goes
out hurriedly, combing his beard*)

IRINA  He's up to something.

TUZENBACH  Yes. He went out looking solemn—plainly,
he's about to bring you a present.

IRINA  What a nuisance!

OLGA  Yes, it's awful. He's always doing something silly.

MASHA  By the curved seastrand a green oak stands, /
A chain of gold upon it . . . (SHE *gets up and hums softly*)

OLGA  You're not very cheerful today, Masha. (MASHA,
*humming, puts on her hat*) Where are you going?

MASHA  Home.

IRINA.  That's strange.

TUZENBACH   To walk out on a birthday party!

MASHA   What's the difference? I'll be back this evening. Good-bye, my darling. . . . (SHE *kisses* IRINA) I'll wish all over again: may you always be well and happy! In the old days, when Father was alive, there'd always be thirty or forty officers here on our birthdays, there was lots of noise, and today there's a man and a half and it's as silent as the tomb. . . . I'm going. I'm depressed today, I feel miserable—don't you listen to me. (SHE *smiles through her tears*) We'll talk afterwards—good-bye till then, dearest, I'm going.

IRINA (*Discontentedly*)   Oh, how can you be so . . .

OLGA (*In tears*)   I understand you, Masha.

SOLYONY   If a man philosophizes, you get philosophy or, anyway, something that looks like philosophy; but if a woman philosophizes, or two do, you might just as well suck your thumb.

MASHA   And what is that supposed to mean, you terribly dreadful man?

SOLYONY   Nothing. Before he'd time to get his breath / The bear was hugging him to death. (*A pause*)

MASHA (*To* OLGA, *angrily*)   Don't sit there sniveling!

[*Enter* ANFISA *and* FERAPONT *with a cake*]

ANFISA   In here, uncle. Come on in, your feet are clean. (*To* IRINA) From the county board, from Mikhail Ivanich Protopopov—a cake.

IRINA   Thank you. And thank him for me, please.

FERAPONT   How's that?

IRINA (*Louder*)   Thank him!

ANFISA   Come on, Ferapont Spiridonich. Come on. . . .

[SHE *goes out with* FERAPONT]

MASHA    I don't like that Protopopov, that Mikhail Potapich or Ivanich or whatever it is. He ought not to be invited.
IRINA    I didn't invite him.
MASHA    That's fine!

[CHEBUTYKIN *enters, behind him an orderly with a silver samovar; there is a hum of amazement and displeasure*]

OLGA (*Covering her face with her hands*)    A samovar! This is awful!

[SHE *goes to the table in the dining room*]

IRINA    Darling Ivan Romanich, what can have possessed you?
TUZENBACH (*Laughing*)    I told you so.
MASHA    Ivan Romanich, you're simply shameless.
CHEBUTYKIN    My darlings, my blessed girls, you are all that I have left, to me you are the most precious treasures that there are upon this earth. Soon I'll be sixty years old: I'm an old man, a lonely worthless old man. The only good that there is in me is my love for you—if it weren't for you I should have left this world long ago. (*To* IRINA) My darling, my own little girl, I've known you since the day you were born. . . . I carried you in these arms. . . . I loved your sainted mother. . . .
IRINA    But why such expensive presents?
CHEBUTYKIN (*Through his tears, angrily*)    Expensive presents! Oh, get out! (*To the* ORDERLY) Carry the samovar over there. (*Mimicking*) Expensive presents!

[*The* ORDERLY *carries the samovar into the dining room*]

ANFISA (*Walking through the living room*)   My dears, there's a strange colonel. He's already taken off his overcoat, children, he's coming in here. Irina darling, now you be a nice polite little girl. (*As* SHE *goes out*) And it was time for lunch hours ago. . . . The Lord have mercy!

TUZENBACH   It must be Vershinin.

[VERSHININ *enters*]

TUZENBACH   Lieutenant Colonel Vershinin!

VERSHININ   I have the honor of introducing myself: Vershinin. I'm so glad, so very glad to be here in your house at last. But how you've grown! My, my!

IRINA   Do sit down. We're delighted.

VERSHININ   How glad I am! How glad I am! But surely there are three of you sisters. I remember—three little girls. I can't remember your faces any longer, but your father, Colonel Prozorov, had three little girls—that I remember distinctly; I saw them with my own eyes. How time does fly! My, my, how time does fly!

TUZENBACH   Alexander Ignatyevich is from Moscow.

IRINA   From Moscow? You're from Moscow?

VERSHININ   Yes, from Moscow. Your father, God bless him, was a battery commander there, and I was an officer in the same brigade. (*To* MASHA) Now that I—it seems to me I do remember your face a little.

MASHA   Yours—I—no!

IRINA   Olga! Olga! (SHE *calls into the dining room*) Olga! Come here!

[OLGA *comes in from the dining room*]

IRINA  It seems Colonel Vershinin's from Moscow.

VERSHININ  You must be Olga Sergeevna, the eldest. . . .
And you're Marya. . . . And you're Irina, the youngest.

OLGA  You're from Moscow?

VERSHININ  Yes, I went to school in Moscow and went
into the service in Moscow, I was stationed there for
many years, and finally they gave me a battery here and
I've moved here, as you see. I don't exactly remember
you, I just remember that there were you three sisters.
But I remember your father so well: if I shut my eyes I
can see him standing there as plain as life. I used to come
to see you in Moscow. . . .

OLGA  It seemed to me I remembered everybody, and
now all at once. . . .

VERSHININ  My name is Alexander Ignatyevich.

IRINA  Alexander Ignatyevich, so you're from Moscow!
What a surprise!

OLGA  We're about to move there, you know.

IRINA  We'll be there by this fall, we expect. It's our
home town, we were born there. . . . On Old Basmanny
Street. (THEY *both laugh with delight*)

MASHA  We've met someone from home—and so unexpectedly! (*Animatedly*) Now I remember! Remember,
Olga, they used to talk to us about "the love-sick major."
You were a lieutenant then, and in love with somebody,
and for some reason they'd all call you major to tease you.

VERSHININ (*Laughing*)  That's it! That's it! The love-
sick major. That was it!

MASHA  You just had a moustache then. But how old
you've got! (*Tearfully*) How old you've got!

VERSHININ  Yes, when they used to call me the love-sick
major I was young, I was in love. It's different now.

OLGA  But you still haven't a single gray hair. You've got older, but you're still not old.

VERSHININ  Just the same, I'm forty-two. Has it been long since you left Moscow?

IRINA  Eleven years. Oh, Masha, what are you crying for, you crazy thing? (*Through her tears*) You've made me cry, too.

MASHA  I'm all right. What street did you live on?

VERSHININ  On Old Basmanny.

OLGA  We did, too.

VERSHININ  For a while I lived on Nyemetski Street. From there I used to go back and forth to the Red Barracks. On the way there's a gloomy-looking bridge, you can hear the water under it. A lonely man gets melancholy there. (*A pause*) But here you've such a broad, such a splendid river! A wonderful river!

OLGA  Yes . . . only it's so cold. It's so cold here, and there're mosquitoes.

VERSHININ  How can you say that? You have such a splendid, healthy, Russian climate here. The forest, the river . . . and there're birches here, too. Dear, modest birches—of all the trees I love birches best. It's good to live here. The only queer thing, the railroad station is ten miles away. . . . And nobody knows why.

SOLYONY  I know why. (EVERYONE *looks at him*) Because if the station were here it wouldn't be way off there; and if it's way off there, then of course it can't be here. (*An awkward silence*)

TUZENBACH  He's a joker, Vasili Vasilich.

OLGA  Now I've remembered you. I remember.

VERSHININ  I knew your mother.

CHEBUTYKIN  She was a lovely woman, bless her soul.

IRINA   Mother is buried in Moscow.

OLGA   In the Novo Devichy. . . .

MASHA   Imagine, I'm already beginning to forget her face. And the same way, they won't remember us. They'll forget us.

VERSHININ   Yes. They'll forget us. That is our fate, there is nothing we can do about it. Everything that seems to us serious, significant, profoundly important—the time will come when it will be forgotten or will seem unimportant. . . . (*A pause*) And what's so interesting is that there's no way for us to know what it is that's going to seem great and important, and what it is that's going to seem pitiful and ridiculous. Take Copernicus or Columbus, for instance—didn't their discoveries seem useless or ridiculous at first, and some fool's empty nonsense seem the truth? And it may be that the life we lead now, the life we reconcile ourselves to so easily, will seem strange some day, uncomfortable, unintelligent, not clean enough—perhaps, even, wrong.

TUZENBACH   Who knows? Or perhaps our life will be called great and be remembered with respect. We don't torture people any more, we've no more executions and invasions—but just the same, how much suffering there is still!

SOLYONY   (*In a high-pitched voice*)   He-ere, chicky, chicky, chicky! Don't feed the baron chicken feed, just let him philosophize.

TUZENBACH   Vasili Vasilich, leave me alone, please. (*He sits down in another place*) After all, this sort of thing gets to be boring.

SOLYONY   (*In a high-pitched voice*)   *He-ere*, chicky, chicky, **chicky**!

TUZENBACH  The suffering we see now—there's still so
much of it—itself is a sign that our society has reached a
certain level of moral development. . . .

VERSHININ  Yes, yes, of course.

CHEBUTYKIN  You said just now, Baron, that they'll call
our life great: just the same, people are very small.
(HE *stands up*) Look how small I am. If anybody were
to say that my life is something great, something that
makes sense, he'd just be saying it to make me feel good.

[*Behind the scene someone is playing the violin*]

MASHA  That's Andrei playing, our brother.

IRINA  He's the scholar of the family. We expect he'll
be a professor someday. Father was a military man, but his
son has chosen an academic career.

MASHA  Father wanted him to.

OLGA  We've been teasing him all morning. It looks as
if he's a little bit in love.

IRINA  With one of the local girls. She'll probably be here
before long.

MASHA  The way she does dress! It's not that her clothes
are ugly or old-fashioned, somehow they're just pathetic.
Some sort of queer gaudy yellowish skirt with a cheap
fringe on it—and a red blouse. And her cheeks scrubbed
till they shine! Andrei isn't in love with her—I refuse
to admit it, he does have some taste—he's just making fun
of us, playing some sort of joke on us. I heard yesterday
that she's going to marry Protopopov, the chairman of
the county board. That would be perfect. (*Through the
side door*) Andrei, come in here! Just for a minute, darling!

[ANDREI *enters*]

OLGA   This is my brother, Andrei Sergeeich.
VERSHININ   Vershinin.
ANDREI   Prozorov. (HE *wipes the sweat off his face*)
You're our new battery commander?
OLGA   Just imagine, Alexander Ignatich is from Moscow.
ANDREI   You are? Well then, I congratulate you—my
sisters won't give you a moment's peace.
VERSHININ   I've already succeeded in boring your sisters.
IRINA   Look at the frame Andrei gave me today!
(*Showing the frame*) He made it himself.
VERSHININ (*Looking at the frame and not knowing what
to say*)   Yes. It's . . . it's a thing . . .

[ANDREI *waves his hand in disgust and walks away*]

OLGA   He's our scholar, and he plays the violin, and
he can make *anything* with his fretsaw. In fact, he's a kind
of universal expert. Don't go away, Andrei! That's the
way he is, always going off by himself. Come back here!

[MASHA *and* IRINA *take him by the arms and, laughing,
lead him back*]

MASHA   Come along! Come along!
ANDREI   Please let me alone.
MASHA   Isn't he absurd! They used to call Alexander
Ignatevich the love-sick major, and he never got angry,
not even once.
VERSHININ   Not even once!
MASHA   I think we ought to call you the love-sick violinist!
IRINA   Or the love-sick professor!
OLGA   He's in love! Our little Andrei's in love!
IRINA (*Applauding*)   Bravo! Bravo! Encore! Our little
Andrei's in love!

CHEBUTYKIN (*Coming up behind* ANDREI *and putting both hands around his waist*) Male and female created He them! (HE *laughs.* HE *still has the newspaper.*)

ANDREI Well, that's enough, that's enough. . . . (HE *wipes his face*) I couldn't sleep all night and this morning I'm not quite myself, as the phrase goes. I read till four o'clock and then went to bed, but it wasn't any use. I'd think of something, and then think of something else— and it gets light so early here: the sunlight simply pours into my bedroom. This summer while I'm here there's this English book I want to translate . . .

VERSHININ You read English?

ANDREI Yes. Father, God bless him, absolutely loaded us down with education. It's absurd, it's idiotic, but just the same I've got to admit that after his death I began to gain weight—in a year I've got fat like this, just as if my body had taken the chance to break loose from him. Thanks to Father my sisters and I know French, German, and English, and Irina even knows Italian. But what's the use of that?

MASHA In this town knowing three languages is a useless luxury. Not even a luxury but a sort of useless appendage, like a sixth finger. We know a lot that isn't any use.

VERSHININ Really now! (HE *laughs*) You know a lot that isn't any use! I don't think that there is a town, that there can be a town, so boring and so dismal that it doesn't need intelligent, cultivated people. Suppose that among the hundred thousand inhabitants of this town— this obviously crude, obviously backward place—suppose that there're only three people like you. It's plain that you won't be able to get the better of the darkness and ignorance around you; as you go on living, little by little

you'll have to give up, you'll be lost in this crowd of a
hundred thousand human beings, their life will choke
you out. But you'll have been here, you'll not disappear
without a trace: later on others like you will come, perhaps
only six at first, then twenty, and so on, until at last people
like you will be in the majority. In two or three hundred
years life on earth will be unimaginably beautiful, unimaginably wonderful. Mankind needs such a life—and
if it isn't here yet then we must look forward to it, wait,
dream of it, prepare for it; and to do that we must see
and know more than our fathers and grandfathers saw
and knew. (HE *laughs*) And you say you know a lot
that isn't any use!

MASHA (*Taking off her hat*)   I'm staying to lunch.

IRINA (*Sighing*)   Really, all that ought to be written down.

[ANDREI *is not there;* HE *has gone out unnoticed*]

TUZENBACH   After many years, you say, life on earth
will be beautiful, wonderful. That is true. But to have a
share in it now, even from a distance, we must get ready
for it, we must work.

VERSHININ   Yes. (HE *gets up*) But what a lot of flowers
you have! (HE *looks around*) And this beautiful house.
I envy you! My whole life has been spent in little apart-
ments with two chairs, a sofa, and a stove that keeps
smoking all the time. It's just such flowers as these that
have been missing in my life. (HE *rubs his hands together*)
Well, there's nothing to be done about it now. . . .

TUZENBACH   Yes, we must work. Probably you're
thinking: the German is getting sentimental. But I give
you my word of honor, I'm Russian, I can't even speak
German. My father's Orthodox. . . (*A pause*)

VERSHININ   I often think, suppose it were possible for
us to begin life over again—and consciously, this time. If
only the first life, the one we've lived through already,
were a rough draft, so to speak, and the other the final
copy! I believe that each of us would try above all not
to repeat himself—or at least would create a different set of
circumstances for his life, would manage to live in a
house like this, with flowers, with plenty of light. . . . I
have a wife and two little girls, and not only that, my wife's
an invalid, and so forth and so on—well, if I were to
begin life over again, I'd never get married. . . . Never,
never!

[KULYGIN *enters, in a schoolteacher's uniform*]

KULYGIN (*Going up to* IRINA)   Dear sister, allow me to
congratulate you on the day of your birth—and to wish for
you, sincerely and from the bottom of my heart, health
and everything else that's appropriate for a girl of your
age. And to offer you as a gift this little book. (HE *hands
her a book*) An insignificant little book, written only
because I had nothing else to do, but just the same, read it.
Good morning, gentlemen! (*To* VERSHININ) Kulygin,
teacher in the local high school, court councillor. (*To*
IRINA) In this book you will find a list of everyone who
has graduated from our high school in the last fifty years.
*Feci, quod potui, faciant meliora potentes.* (HE *kisses*
MASHA)
IRINA   But you gave me one Easter!
KULYGIN (HE *laughs*)   Impossible! Well, in that case
give it back—or better still, give it to the colonel. Take it,
Colonel. Some day when you're bored, read it.

VERSHININ Thank you. (HE *is about to leave*) I'm
extremely glad to have made your acquaintance—
OLGA You're leaving? No, no!
IRINA Surely you'll stay and have lunch with us. Please.
OLGA I beg you.
VERSHININ I can see I've happened in on a party for
your birthday. Forgive me, I didn't know—I haven't
congratulated you.

[HE *goes into the dining room with* OLGA]

KULYGIN Today, gentlemen, is a Sunday, a day of rest,
so let us rest, let us rejoice, each in accordance with his
age and position. The rugs must be taken up for the
summer and put away till winter . . . with moth balls or
naphthalene. . . . The Romans were healthy because
they knew both how to work and how to rest, they had
*mens sana in corpore sano.* Their lives were organized
into a definite routine. Our principal is fond of saying
that the most important thing in any life is its routine.
. . . That which loses its routine loses its very existence—
and it is exactly the same in our everyday life. (HE *takes*
MASHA *by the waist, laughing*) Masha loves me. My wife
loves me. And the curtains too, along with the carpets.
. . . I am gay today, in the very best of spirits. Masha,
at four o'clock today we are due at the principal's. An
outing has been arranged for the teachers and their
families.
MASHA I'm not going.
KULYGIN (*Aggrieved*) But dear Masha, why?
MASHA We'll talk about it later. . . . (*Angrily*) Oh, all
right, I'll go, only please leave me alone. . . .

[SHE *walks away*]

KULYGIN   And afterwards we're to spend the evening at the principal's. In spite of the precarious condition of his health, that man tries above all else to be sociable. A stimulating, an outstanding personality! Yesterday after the faculty meeting he said to me: "I am tired, Fyodor Ilich! I am tired!" (HE *looks at the clock on the wall, then at his watch*) Your clock is seven minutes fast. "Yes," he said, "I am tired!"

[*Behind the scene a violin is playing*]

OLGA   Ladies and gentlemen, please come to lunch. There's a meat pie.

KULYGIN   Ah, Olga, my dear Olga! Yesterday I worked from early morning till eleven o'clock at night, and I was tired, literally exhausted—and today I am happy. (HE *goes into the dining room by the table*) Ah, my dear . . .

CHEBUTYKIN (*Putting the newspaper into his pocket and combing his beard*)   A meat pie? Splendid!

MASHA (*To Chebutykin, sternly*)   Only—listen to me!— nothing to drink today. Do you hear? It's bad for you.

CHEBUTYKIN   Oh, come on, that's ancient history. I haven't been drunk for two years. (*Impatiently*) And, my dear girl, what's the difference anyway?

MASHA   Difference or no difference, don't you dare drink! Don't you dare! (*Angrily, but so that her husband doesn't hear*) Oh, damnation, damnation! for another whole evening to sit and be bored to death at that principal's!

TUZENBACH   If I were you I just wouldn't go. It's perfectly simple.

CHEBUTYKIN   Don't you go, my darling!

MASHA   Yes, don't you go! . . . A damnable life! an insufferable life!

[SHE *goes into the dining room*]

CHEBUTYKIN (*Going after her*)   Now, now!
SOLYONY (*Going into the dining room*)   He-ere, chicky, chicky, chicky!
TUZENBACH   That's enough, Vasili Vasilich. Stop it!
SOLYONY   *He-ere*, chicky, chicky, chicky!
KULYGIN (*Cheerfully*)   Your health, Colonel! I am a pedagogue, you know, and here in this house I'm one of the family, Masha's husband. . . . She is kind—so kind. . . .
VERSHININ   I'll have some of this dark vodka here. (*Drinking*) Your health! (*To* OLGA) I feel so good here at your house! . . .

[*Only* IRINA *and* TUZENBACH *are left in the living room*]

IRINA   Masha's not in a very good humor today. She was married when she was eighteen, and he seemed to her the most intelligent of men. It's different now. He's the kindest of men, but not the most intelligent.
OLGA (*Impatiently*)   Andrei, *please* come on. After all! . . .
ANDREI (*Offstage*)   This minute.

[HE *comes in and goes over to the table*]

TUZENBACH   What are you thinking about?
IRINA   This: I don't like that Solyony of yours, I'm afraid of him. Everything he says is so stupid. . . .
TUZENBACH   He's a strange man. I'm sorry for him and irritated at him too, but mostly I'm sorry for him. It seems to me he's shy. . . . When he's alone with you he's quite intelligent and pleasant, but when there're other

people around he's rude, a sort of bully. Don't go, let's
let them sit down without us. Let me be near you a little.
What are you thinking about? (*A pause*) You're twenty,
I'm not thirty yet. How many years we still have left—
so many days, row on row of them, all full of my love
for you. . . .

IRINA  Nikolai Lvovich, don't talk to me about love.

TUZENBACH (*Not listening*)  I long so passionately to live,
to struggle, to work—and because I love you, Irina, the
longing's stronger than ever: it's as if you were meant
to be so beautiful, and life seems to me just as beautiful.
What are you thinking about?

IRINA  You say life is beautiful. Yes, but suppose it only
seems that way! For us three sisters life hasn't been
beautiful, it's—it's choked us out, the way weeds choke
out grass. I'm crying. . . . (SHE *quickly wipes her eyes
and smiles*) I mustn't cry. We must work, work. We're so
unhappy, we take such a gloomy view of life, because
we don't work. We come from people who despised work.

[NATALYA (NATASHA) IVANOVNA *enters;* SHE *has on a
pink dress and a bright green belt*]

NATASHA  They've already sat down to the table. . . .
I'm late. . . . (*As* SHE *goes by it* SHE *looks into the mirror
and tidies herself*) My hair seems to be all right. . . .
(*Seeing* IRINA) Many happy returns of the day, dear Irina
Sergeevna! (SHE *gives her a vigorous and prolonged kiss*)
You've got such a lot of visitors, I really do feel em-
barrassed. . . . How do you do, Baron!

OLGA (*Entering the living room*)  Why, here's Natalya
Ivanovna! How are you, dear?

[THEY *kiss*]

NATASHA Many happy returns! You've got so much company I really do feel terribly embarrassed.

OLGA You mustn't, it's only the family. (*In an undertone, alarmed*) You have on a green belt! Dear, that's too bad—

NATASHA What's wrong, is it bad luck?

OLGA No, it's just that it doesn't go with . . . somehow it looks a little strange.

NATASHA (*In a tearful voice*) It—it does? But it isn't really green, it's more a sort of a neutral shade.

[SHE *follows* OLGA *into the dining room.*
*In the dining room* THEY *sit down to lunch; there is no one left in the living room.*]

KULYGIN I wish you, Irina, a good fiancé! It's time you were getting married.

CHEBUTYKIN Natalya Ivanovna, I wish you a fiancé too.

KULYGIN Natalya Ivanovna already has a fiancé.

MASHA I'll have a little drink! What the—life's a bed of roses! Come on, take a chance!

KULYGIN For that you get a C-minus in deportment.

VERSHININ This liqueur's good—what's it made of?

SOLYONY Cockroaches.

IRINA Ugh! How disgusting!

OLGA For dinner we're having roast turkey and apple pie. Thank the Lord, I'll be home all day today and home all evening. Everybody must come this evening.

VERSHININ Let me come this evening, too.

OLGA Please do.

NATASHA They certainly don't wait to be asked twice around here.

CHEBUTYKIN   Male and female created He them! (HE *laughs*)

ANDREI (*Angrily*)   Oh, stop it, everybody! Don't you ever get tired of it?

[FEDOTIK *and* RODE *enter with a big basket of flowers*]

FEDOTIK   Look, they're already having lunch. . . .
RODE (*Loudly and affectedly*)   Already having lunch? That's right, they're already having lunch.
FEDOTIK   Hold still a minute! (HE *takes a photograph*) One! Wait, just one more! (HE *takes another photograph*) Two! Now it's all right.

[THEY *pick up the basket and go on into the dining room, where* THEY *are greeted noisily*]

RODE (*Loudly*)   Many happy returns! I wish you everything, everything! It's wonderful out today, absolutely magnificent. I've been out all morning with the high school boys, on a hike. I teach the gym class at the high school, you know.
FEDOTIK   You can move, Irina Sergeevna, you can move now. (HE *takes a photograph*) You look simply beautiful today. (HE *takes a top out of his pocket*) By the way, here's a little top. . . . It makes the most wonderful sound. . . .
IRINA   How *nice*!
MASHA   By the curved sea-strand a green oak stands,
A chain of gold upon it . . .
A chain of gold upon it . . . (*Tearfully*) What am I saying that for? It's been going through my head all day. . . .
KULYGIN   Thirteen at table!
RODE (*Loudly*)   But surely, ladies and gentlemen, you

do not actually take such superstitions as these seriously?
(*Laughter*)

KULYGIN   If there're thirteen at table it means that one
of them's in love. It's not you by any chance, Ivan
Romanovich? (*Laughter*)

CHEBUTYKIN   I'm an old reprobate, but why Natalya
Ivanovna is so embarrassed I simply can't imagine.

[*Loud laughter.* NATALYA *runs out of the dining room
into the living room;* ANDREI *follows her.*]

ANDREI   Please don't pay any attention to them! Wait. . . .
Don't go, please don't. . . .

NATASHA   I'm ashamed. . . . I don't know what's the
matter with me, and they're all making fun of me. I know
it's bad manners for me to leave the table like this, but I
just can't help it. . . . I just can't. . . .

(SHE *covers her face with her hands*)

ANDREI   Dear, I beg you, I implore you, don't let them
upset you. Honestly, they're only joking, they mean
well. They have such kind hearts—my darling, my dearest,
they're all such good, kindhearted people, they love both
of us. Come over here by the window, they can't see
us here. . . . (HE *looks around*)

NATASHA   I'm just not used to being in society!

ANDREI   Ah, youth, marvelous, beautiful youth! My
darling, my dearest, please don't be upset! Believe me,
believe me. . . . I'm so happy, so in love—I'm so blissfully
happy. . . . Oh, they can't see us! They can't see us at all!
Why I first fell in love with you, when I first fell in love
with you—I don't know . . . My dearest, my darling, my

innocent one, be my wife! I love you, love you as nobody
ever—

    [THEY *kiss.*
    Two OFFICERS *come in and seeing the two kissing,
stop in amazement.*]

CURTAIN

# ACT II

THE SCENE IS THAT OF THE FIRST ACT. IT IS EIGHT o'clock at night. The faint sound of an accordion comes up from the street. The room is dark. NATALYA IVANOVNA enters in a dressing gown, with a candle; SHE walks over and stops at the door of ANDREI'S room.

NATASHA  Andrei . . . dear, what are you doing? Reading? Nothing, I just . . . (SHE goes to another door, opens it, looks inside, and then shuts it) No, there isn't one. . . .
ANDREI (Entering with a book in his hand) What, Natasha?
NATASHA  I was looking to see whether there's a light. . . . Now it's carnival week the servants are simply impossible, you have to be on the lookout every minute to make sure nothing goes wrong. Last night at midnight I went through the dining room, and there on the table was a lighted candle! Now, who lit it? I still haven't been able to get a straight answer. (SHE puts down her candle) What time is it?
ANDREI (Looking at his watch) Quarter after eight.
NATASHA  And Olga and Irina not in yet. They aren't in yet. Still hard at work, poor things! Olga at the teachers' council and Irina at the telegraph office. . . . (SHE sighs) I was saying to your sister just this morning, "Irina

darling," I said, "you simply must take better care of
yourself." But she just won't listen. . . . Quarter after
eight, you said? I'm worried, I'm afraid our Bobik just
isn't well. Why is he so cold? Yesterday he had a
temperature and today he's cold all over. . . . I am so
worried!

ANDREI   It's all right, Natasha. The boy's all right.

NATASHA   Just the same, I think we'd better put him on a
diet. I *am* worried. And tonight at almost ten o'clock
those carnival people are going to be here, they said—
it would be better if they didn't come, Andrei dear.

ANDREI   I don't know. They *have* been asked, you know.

NATASHA   This morning the little thing woke up and
looked at me, and all of a sudden he gave a big smile: he
knew me! "Good morning, Bobik!" I said. "Good morning,
sweetheart!" And he laughed. . . . Babies understand,
they understand perfectly. So Andrei dear, I'm going to
tell them they mustn't let those carnival people in.

ANDREI   (*Indecisively*)   But that's up to my sisters, you
know. This is their house.

NATASHA   Yes, theirs too. I'll speak to them. They're so
kind. . . . (SHE *starts to leave*) I've ordered cottage cheese
for your supper. The doctor says you mustn't eat anything but cottage cheese or you won't ever get any
thinner. (SHE *stops*) Bobik is *cold*. I'm afraid he must be
cold in that room of his. At least till it's warm weather,
we ought to put him in a different room. For instance,
Irina's room is a perfect room for a child, it's dry and
the sun simply pours in all day long. I must speak to her
about it. She could stay in Olga's room with her, for the
time being. . . . It won't make any difference to her,
she's never at home in the daytime anyway, she only

*Masha and Vershinin*
Photograph by FRIEDMAN-ABELES

spends the night there. . . . (*A pause*) Andrei-Wandrei,
why don't you say something?
ANDREI  I was just thinking. . . . Anyway, there isn't
anything to say. . . .
NATASHA  Uh-huh. . . . There was something I meant to
tell you about. . . . Now I remember: Ferapont's here
from the county board, he wants to see you.
ANDREI  (*Yawning*)  Send him on in.

[NATASHA *goes out.* ANDREI, *stooping over the candle.*
SHE *has left, reads his book.* FERAPONT *comes in;* HE
*is in a worn-out old overcoat, the collar turned up, a
scarf over his ears.*]

ANDREI  How are you, Ferapont, old man? What have
you got to tell me?
FERAPONT  The chairman's sent you a little book and
some kind of paper. Here . . . (HE *gives a book and an
envelope to* ANDREI)
ANDREI  Thanks. That's fine. But what did you come so
late for? It's already past eight, you know.
FERAPONT  How's that?
ANDREI  (*Louder*)  I said you're late, it's past eight.
FERAPONT  That's right. I got here when it was still
light but they wouldn't let me in. The master's busy, they
said. Well, if you're busy you're busy, I'm not in any
hurry. (*Thinking that* ANDREI *has said something*) How's
that?
ANDREI  Nothing. (HE *examines the book*) Tomorrow's
Friday, we don't have any meeting, but I'll come anyway. . . . I'll do something. It's boring at home. (*A pause*)
Ferapont, old man, it's funny how life changes, how it
fools you. Today out of pure boredom, just because I

hadn't anything else to do, I picked up this book here, some old university lectures, and I couldn't help laughing. . . . Good God! I'm the secretary of the county board, the board Protopopov's the head of; I'm the secretary, and the very most I can ever hope for is—to be a member of the board! I a member of a county board—I who dream every night that I'm a professor at the University of Moscow, a famous scholar of whom all Russia is proud!

FERAPONT    I couldn't rightly say . . . I'm a little hard of hearing. . . .

ANDREI    If you could hear as you ought I might not be talking to you like this. I've got to talk to somebody and my wife doesn't understand me, I'm afraid of my sisters, somehow—I'm afraid they'll make fun of me, make me feel ashamed. . . . You know, I don't drink, I don't like cafés, but . . . good old Ferapont, what I'd give to be sitting in Moscow right now, at Testov's or the Great Muscovite!

FERAPONT    In Moscow, there was a contractor at the board the other day that said so, there were some merchants eating pancakes, and it seems as how one of them ate forty pancakes and he died. It was either forty or fifty. I don't remember.

ANDREI    In Moscow you sit in the main room at a restaurant, you don't know anybody and nobody knows you, but just the same you don't feel like a stranger. And here you know everybody and everybody knows you, and you're a stranger, a stranger . . . a stranger and lonely.

FERAPONT    How's that? (*A pause*) And the contractor

said—maybe he was lying, though—that there's a rope
stretched all the way across Moscow.

ANDREI   What for?

FERAPONT   I couldn't rightly say. The contractor said so.

ANDREI   That's nonsense. (HE *reads*) Have you ever
been to Moscow?

FERAPONT (*After a pause*)   I never have. It wasn't God's
will I should. (*A pause*) Shall I go now?

ANDREI   You can go. Good-bye. (FERAPONT *goes out*)
Good-bye. (*Reading*) In the morning come back and
get these papers. . . . You can go. . . . (*A pause*) He's
gone. (*The bell rings*) Yes, it's a nuisance. . . .

[HE *stretches and walks slowly into his room.
Behind the scene the* NURSE *is singing, rocking the
baby.* MASHA *and* VERSHININ *enter. While* THEY *talk,
a* MAID *is lighting the lamp and candles.*]

MASHA   I don't know. (*A pause*) I don't know. Of course,
a lot of it is just habit. For instance, after Father's death
it took us a long time to get used to not having orderlies
in the house. But even if you disregard habit, it's only fair
to say that—maybe it's not so in other places—that in
our town the nicest people, the decentest people, the
best-mannered people, really are the ones in the army.

VERSHININ   I'm thirsty. I'd certainly like some tea.

MASHA   It'll be here before long. They married me when
I was eighteen, and I was afraid of my husband because
he was a teacher and I was barely out of school. He
seemed terribly learned to me then, intelligent, and important. It's different now, unfortunately.

VERSHININ   I see . . . yes.

MASHA   I'm not talking about my husband, I'm used to him, but among civilians in general there're so many coarse, unpleasant, ill-bred people. Coarseness upsets me—insults me; when I see that a man isn't polite enough, isn't refined or delicate enough, I suffer. When I'm with the teachers, my husband's colleagues, I'm simply miserable.

VERSHININ   Yes. . . . But it seems to me it doesn't make any difference—whether they're army men or civilians, they're equally uninteresting . . . in this town, at any rate. It makes no difference! If you listen to one of the local intellectuals, civilian or military, all you ever hear is that he's sick and tired of his wife, sick and tired of his house, sick and tired of his estate, sick and tired of his horses. . . . When it comes to lofty ideas, thinking on an exalted plane, a Russian is extraordinary, but will you tell me why it is he aims so low in life? Why?

MASHA   Why?

VERSHININ   Why is a Russian always sick and tired of his children, sick and tired of his wife? And why are his wife and children always sick and tired of him?

MASHA   You're a little depressed today.

VERSHININ   Perhaps. I didn't have any dinner—I've had nothing to eat since breakfast. One of my daughters isn't exactly well, and when my little girls are ill I get anxious about them, my conscience torments me for having given them such a mother. If you could have seen her today! What a miserable creature! We began quarreling at seven in the morning, and at nine I slammed the door and walked away. . . . (*A pause*) I never mention it to anybody—it's strange, it's only to you that I complain. (*He kisses her hand*) Don't be angry with me. If it weren't for you I'd have no one—no one. (*A pause*)

MASHA   Listen to the chimney! Just before Father died there was a howling in the chimney—there, just like that!

VERSHININ   You're superstitious?

MASHA   Yes.

VERSHININ   That's strange. (HE *kisses her hand*) You're a splendid woman, a wonderful woman. Splendid, wonderful! It's dark in here, but I can see how your eyes sparkle.

MASHA (*Moving to another chair*)   The light's better over here.

VERSHININ   I love, love, love . . . love your eyes, the way you move, I see them in my dreams. . . . Splendid, wonderful woman!

MASHA (*Laughing softly*)   When you talk to me like that, somehow, I don't know why, I laugh, even when it frightens me. But don't do it again, please don't. . . . (*In a low voice*) No, you can, though—it doesn't make any difference to me. . . . (SHE *covers her face with her hands*) It doesn't make any difference to me. Someone's coming. Talk about something else.

[IRINA *and* TUZENBACH *come in through the dining room*]

TUZENBACH   I've got three last names, my name is BARON Tuzenbach-Krone-Altschauer, and yet I'm Russian and Orthodox, just like you. There's hardly anything German left in me—nothing, maybe, except the patience and obstinacy with which I keep boring you. Every single night I see you home.

IRINA   I'm so tired!

TUZENBACH   And every single day for ten years, for twenty years, I'll come to the telegraph office and see you

home, as long as you don't drive me away. . . . (*Seeing*
MASHA *and* VERSHININ, *delightedly*) Oh, it's you! How
are you!

IRINA   Here I am, home at last! (*To* MASHA) Just before
I left a lady came in—she was wiring her brother in
Saratov that her son had died today, and she couldn't
manage to remember the address. So she sent it without
any address, just to Saratov. She was crying. And for no
reason whatsoever, I was rude to her. I said, "I simply
haven't the time." It was so stupid! Are the carnival
people coming tonight?

MASHA   Yes.

IRINA (*Sitting down in an armchair*)   I'll rest. I'm so tired.

TUZENBACH (*Smiling*)   When you come home from
work you seem so young and so unhappy. . . . (*A pause*)

IRINA   I'm tired. No, I don't like working there, I don't
like it.

MASHA   You've got thinner . . . (SHE *begins to whistle*)
And younger, and your face looks like a little boy's.

TUZENBACH   That's the way she does her hair.

IRINA   I must try to find some other job, this one's not
right for me. What I longed for so, what I dreamed about,
is exactly what's missing. It's work without poetry, without sense, even . . . (*A knock on the floor*) The Doctor's
knocking. . . . (*To* TUZENBACH) You knock, dear. . . .
I can't . . . I'm so tired. (TUZENBACH *knocks on the floor*)
He'll be right up. Some way or other we've got to do
something about it. Yesterday he and Andrei were at
the club, and they lost again. They say Andrei lost two
hundred rubles.

MASHA (*Indifferently*)   Well, there's nothing we can
do about it now.

IRINA  Two weeks ago he lost, in December he lost. If only he'd hurry up and lose everything, maybe then we'd get out of this town. My God, every night I dream of Moscow, it's as if I were possessed. (SHE *laughs*) We're moving there in June, from now to June leaves—February, March, April, May . . . almost half a year!

MASHA  The only thing is, Natasha mustn't hear anything about what he's lost.

IRINA  I don't think it makes any difference to her.

[CHEBUTYKIN, *just out of bed—*HE *has taken a nap after dinner—enters the dining room combing his beard, then sits down at the table and takes a newspaper from his pocket*]

MASHA  So, he arrives. . . . Has he paid anything on his apartment?

IRINA (*Laughing*)  No. For eight months, not a kopeck. Evidently he's forgotten.

MASHA (*Laughing*)  How grandly he sits there! (EVERY-BODY *laughs. A pause.*)

IRINA  Why are you so silent, Alexander Ignatich?

VERSHININ  I don't know. I'd like some tea. I'd sell my soul for a glass of tea! I've had nothing to eat since breakfast. . . .

CHEBUTYKIN  Irina Sergeevna!

IRINA  What is it?

CHEBUTYKIN  Please come here. *Venez ici!* (IRINA *goes and sits down at the table*) I simply cannot do without you.

VERSHININ  Well, if they won't give us any tea, at least let's philosophize.

TUZENBACH  Yes, let's. What about?

VERSHININ  What about? Let's dream . . . for instance,

about the life that will come after us, in two or three hundred years.

TUZENBACH   Well, after us they'll fly in balloons, their clothes will be different, they'll discover a sixth sense, maybe and then develop it; but life will stay the same, a difficult life, full of mysteries, and happy. And in a thousand years people will be sighing, the same as now: "Ah, life is hard!"—and along with that, exactly the same as now, they'll be frightened of death and not want to die.

VERSHININ (*After a moment's thought*)   How shall I put it? It seems to me that everything on earth must change, little by little, and that it is already changing before our eyes. In two or three hundred, in a thousand years—the length of time doesn't matter—a new and happy life will come. We can have no share in it, of course, but we are living for it, working for it, yes, suffering for it: we are creating it—and in that and in that alone is the aim of our existence and, if you wish, our happiness. (MASHA *laughs softly*)

TUZENBACH   What's the matter with you?

MASHA   I don't know. All day today, ever since morning, I've been laughing.

VERSHININ   I finished school there where you did, I didn't go on to the Academy; I read a lot, but I don't know how to choose the books, and what I read, maybe, isn't exactly what I need to read. But the longer I live the more I want to know. My hair's getting gray, I'm an old man, almost, and yet I know so little, oh, so little! Still, though, it seems to me that what matters most, what's absolutely essential—that I do know, and know very well. If only I could make you see that there *is* no happiness, that there should not be, and that there will not be, for us. . . . We must only work and work, and happiness— that is the lot of our remote descendants. (*A pause*) Not mine but, at least, that of the descendants of my descendants.

[FEDOTIK *and* RODE *appear in the dining room;* THEY *sit down and softly begin to sing, one of them playing on the guitar*]

TUZENBACH  According to you, we ought not even to dream of happiness! But suppose I *am* happy?
VERSHININ  No.
TUZENBACH (*Throwing up his hands and laughing*) Obviously we don't understand each other. Well, how am I going to convince you? (MASHA *laughs softly*)
TUZENBACH (*Showing her his finger*)  Laugh! (*To* VERSHININ) Not just in two or three hundred but in a million years, even, life will be the same: it doesn't change, it goes on the same as ever, obeying laws of its own— laws that are none of our business or, anyhow, that we'll never be able to discover. Migratory birds, cranes for instance, fly and fly, and no matter what thoughts, great or small, wander into their heads, they'll still keep on flying, they don't know where, they don't know why. They fly and will fly, no matter what philosophers appear among them; and they can philosophize as much as they please, just so long as they still fly.
MASHA  But still, it means something?
TUZENBACH  Means something. . . . Look, it's snowing. What does that mean? (*A pause*)

MASHA   It seems to me a man must believe or search for
some belief, or else his life is empty, empty. . . . To live
and not know why the cranes fly, why children are born,
why there are stars in the sky. . . . Either you know what
you're living for or else it's all nonsense, hocus-pocus.
VERSHININ   Still, it's a pity one's youth is over.
MASHA   Gogol says: Life on this earth is a dull proposition,
gentlemen! I give up.
CHEBUTYKIN (*Reading a newspaper*)   Balzac was married
in Berdichev. (IRINA *softly begins to sing*) I really ought
to write that down in my book. (HE *writes it down*)
Balzac was married in Berdichev. (HE *reads his newspaper*)
IRINA (*Pensively, as* SHE *lays out the cards for solitaire*)
Balzac was married in Berdichev.
TUZENBACH   The die is cast. You know, I've handed in
my resignation, Marya Sergeevna.
MASHA   So I hear. But I don't see anything good about
that. I don't like civilians.
TUZENBACH   What's the difference? . . . (HE *gets up*)
I'm not handsome, what sort of soldier am I? Well,
anyway, what's the difference? . . . I'm going to work. If
only for one day in my life, work so that I come home
at night, fall in bed exhausted, and go right to sleep. (HE
*goes into the dining room*) Surely workmen must sleep
soundly!
FEDOTIK   I got these crayons for you—on Moscow
Street, at Pyzikov's. . . . And this little penknife. . . .
IRINA   You keep on treating me as if I were a little girl,
but I'm grown up now, you know. . . . (*Taking the
crayons and the knife, joyfully*) How lovely!
FEDOTIK   And I bought myself a knife. . . . Look. . . . One

blade, two, three, this is to clean your ears with, a pair of scissors, this is to clean your nails with. . . .

RODE (*Loudly*)   Doctor, how old are you?

CHEBUTYKIN   I? Thirty-two. (*Laughter*)

FEDOTIK   I will now show you a new kind of solitaire. . . .

[HE lays out the cards.

THEY *bring in the samovar;* ANFISA *stands by it; a little later* NATASHA *comes in and begins to straighten things on the table;* SOLYONY *enters, is greeted, and sits down at the table.*]

VERSHININ   What a wind!

MASHA   Yes. I'm bored with winter. I've forgotten what summer's like.

IRINA   I'm going to go out, I can see it. We're going to get to Moscow!

FEDOTIK   No it's not—see, that eight's on the deuce of spades. (*He laughs*) So you're not going to get to Moscow.

CHEBUTYKIN (*Reading the newspaper*) Tsitsikar. Small-pox is raging here.

ANFISA (*Going up to* MASHA) Masha, have some tea, darling. (*To* VERSHININ) Please, your honor. . . . Excuse me, sir, I've forgotten your name. . . .

MASHA   Bring it over here, nurse. I'm not going there.

IRINA   Nurse!

ANFISA   Coming-g!

NATASHA (*To* SOLYONY)   Babies, little babies still at the breast—they understand perfectly. "Good morning, Bobik!" I say. "Good morning, sweetheart!" Then he looks up at me in a very special way. You think I'm just saying that because I'm a mother, but that isn't so, no indeed it isn't so! He really is the most amazing child.

SOLYONY   If that child were mine I'd fry him in a frying pan and then eat him.

[HE *picks up his glass, goes into the living room, and sits down in a corner*]

NATASHA (*Covering her face with her hands*)   Rude, common man!

MASHA   If you're happy you don't notice whether it's summer or winter. It seems to me that if I were in Moscow I wouldn't care what the weather was like.

VERSHININ   The other day I was reading the diary of some French cabinet minister—he's been sent to prison because of that Panama affair. With what rapture, with what delight he describes the birds he sees from the window of his cell . . . birds he'd never noticed in the days when he was a minister. Now that they've let him out again, of course, it's the same as it used to be: he doesn't notice the birds. Just as when you live in Moscow again, you won't notice it. We aren't happy, we never will be, we only long to be.

TUZENBACH (*Picking up a box from the table*)   What's become of the candy?

IRINA   Solyony ate it.

TUZENBACH   All of it?

ANFISA (*Serving tea*)   A letter for you, sir.

VERSHININ   For me? (HE *takes the letter*) From my daughter. (HE *reads*) Yes, of course. . . . Forgive me, Marya Sergeevna, I'll slip out quietly. No tea for me. (HE *gets up, disturbed*) The same old story. . . .

MASHA   What is it? It's not a secret?

VERSHININ (*In a low voice*) My wife's poisoned herself again. I must go. I'll slip out so no one will notice. All this is horribly unpleasant. (HE *kisses* MASHA's *hand*) My good, darling, wonderful woman. . . . I'll just slip out quietly. . . .

ANFISA Where on earth's he going now? After I've poured him out his tea. . . . If he isn't a . . .

MASHA (*Losing her temper*) Stop it! Bothering everybody to death, you never give us a moment's peace. . . . (SHE *goes over to the table with her cup*) I'm bored with you, old woman!

ANFISA What are you so mad about? Darling girl!

ANDREI'S VOICE (*Offstage*) Anfisa!

ANFISA (*Mimicking him*) Anfisa! There he sits . . .

[SHE *goes out*]

MASHA (*By the table in the dining room, angrily*) Let me sit down! (SHE *mixes up the cards on the table*) Sprawling all over the place with your cards. Drink your tea!

IRINA Masha, you're just mean.

MASHA Well if I'm mean don't talk to me. Don't bother me!

CHEBUTYKIN (*Laughing*) Don't bother her, don't bother her. . . .

MASHA You're sixty years old and yet you behave like a spoiled child, always jabbering the devil knows what. . . .

NATASHA (SHE *sighs*) Dear Masha, why *must* you use such expressions in conversation? With your looks you'd be simply fascinating in society if only it weren't for these—I'm going to be frank with you—for these expressions of yours. Excuse me for mentioning it, Masha, but your manners *are* a little coarse.

TUZENBACH (*Trying to keep from laughing*)   Give
me . . . Give me . . . It seems to me there's some cognac
somewhere. . . .

NATASHA   It looks like my little Bobik isn't asleep any
more, he's waked up. He isn't well today. I must go to
him, excuse me. . . .

[SHE *goes out*]

IRINA   And where's Alexander Ignatich gone?

MASHA   Home. Something about his wife again—something odd.

TUZENBACH (*Going over to* SOLYONY *with a decanter of
cognac*)   You always sit by yourself thinking about
something, and there's no telling what it is. Come on, let's
make peace. Let's have some cognac. (THEY *drink*) I'll
have to play the piano all night tonight, I expect—all sorts
of trash. . . . Well, come what may!

SOLYONY   Why make peace? I'm not mad at you.

TUZENBACH   You always give me the feeling that something's gone wrong between us. You're a strange character, you've got to admit it.

SOLYONY (*Declaiming*)   I am strange, and yet, who is not
strange? Ah, be not wroth, Aleko!

TUZENBACH   You see! How'd that Aleko get in? (*A pause*)

SOLYONY   When I'm alone with anybody I'm all right,
I'm just like everybody else, but when there are people
around I get depressed and shy and . . . just talk nonsense.
But just the same, I'm more honest and sincere than lots
of people—lots and lots of people. And I can prove it.

TUZENBACH   I'm always getting angry at you, you keep
bothering me so when there're other people around,

but I like you just the same . . . why I don't know. . . .
Come what may, I'm going to get drunk tonight. Let's
have another!

SOLYONY Yes, let's! (HE *drinks*) I never have had anything against you, Baron. But I have a disposition like
Lermontov's. . . . (*In a low voice*) I even look a little like
Lermontov . . . so I'm told. . . . (HE *takes a bottle of
perfume from his pocket and sprinkles some over his hands*)

TUZENBACH I've sent in my resignation. Finished! For
five years I've been thinking about it and at last I've made
up my mind. I'm going to work.

SOLYONY (*Declaiming*) Ah, be not wroth, Aleko. . . .
Forget, forget thy dreams. . . .

[*While* THEY *are talking* ANDREI *comes in quietly, a
book in his hand, and sits down by a candle*]

TUZENBACH I'm going to work.

CHEBUTYKIN (*Coming into the living room with* IRINA)
And besides that, they had real Caucasian food for me—
onion soup, and for the meat course *chekhartma*.

SOLYONY *Cheremsha* isn't meat at all, it's a vegetable
like an onion.

CHEBUTYKIN No indeed, my angel. . . . *Chekhartma*
isn't onion, it's roast lamb.

SOLYONY And I tell you, *cheremsha*'s onion.

CHEBUTYKIN And I tell you, *chekhartma*'s lamb.

SOLYONY And I tell you, *cheremsha*'s onion.

CHEBUTYKIN What's the use of arguing with you! You
never were in the Caucasus, you never ate any *chekhartma*.

SOLYONY I never ate it because I hate it. *Cheremsha*
smells—it smells like garlic.

ANDREI (*Imploringly*)   That's enough, gentlemen! I beg you.

TUZENBACH   When are the carnival people coming?

IRINA   They promised about nine—and that means any minute.

TUZENBACH (*Embracing* ANDREI *and singing*)   "O my porch, O my porch, O my new porch . . ."

ANDREI (*Dancing and singing*)   "My new porch, my maple porch . . ."

CHEBUTYKIN (*Dancing*)   "Porch with my new trellis!" (*Laughter*)

TUZENBACH (*Embracing* ANDREI)   Ah, the devil take it, let's have a drink! Old Andrei, let's drink to our eternal friendship! And Andrei, I'm going right along to Moscow with you, to the University.

SOLYONY   To which university? There's two universities in Moscow.

ANDREI   There's one university in Moscow.

SOLYONY   And I tell you, there're two.

ANDREI   There can be three for all I care. The more the better.

SOLYONY   There're two universities in Moscow! (*Murmurs of protest; people say, "Ssh!"*) There're two universities in Moscow, the old one and the new one. And if you don't want to listen to me, if my words annoy you, then I don't have to talk. I can even go in the other room. . . .

[HE *goes out through one of the doors*]

TUZENBACH   Bravo, bravo! (HE *laughs*) Get ready, ladies and gentlemen, I'm about to sit down at the piano! That Solyony, he's a funny one!

[HE *sits down at the piano and plays a waltz*]

MASHA (*Waltzing by herself*)   The Ba-ron's drunk, the
Ba-ron's drunk, the Ba-a-ron is dru-unk! (NATASHA
*comes in*)
NATASHA (*To* CHEBUTYKIN) Ivan Romanich!

[SHE *speaks about something with* CHEBUTYKIN, *then
quietly goes out.* CHEBUTYKIN *touches* TUZENBACH *on
the shoulder and whispers to him.*]

IRINA   What's the matter?
CHEBUTYKIN   It's time we were going. Good-bye.
TUZENBACH   Good night. Time we were going.
IRINA   But—but what do you mean? What about the
carnival people?
ANDREI (*Embarrassed*)   There aren't going to be any
carnival people. You see, my dear, Natasha says that Bobik
doesn't feel very good, and so . . . To tell the truth, I
don't know anything about it, it doesn't make any difference to me.
IRINA (*Shrugging her shoulders*)   Bobik doesn't feel good!
MASHA   Oh, what's the difference! If they run us out,
then we've got to go. (*To* IRINA) There's nothing wrong
with Bobik, there's something wrong with her. . . . Here!
(SHE *taps her forehead*) Common little creature!

[ANDREI *goes into his room;* CHEBUTYKIN *follows him;
in the dining room* THEY *are saying good-bye*]

FEDOTIK   What a shame! I was counting on spending
the evening, but if the little baby's sick then of course . . .
Tomorrow I'll bring him a little toy. . . .

RODE (*Loudly*)   I took a long nap this afternoon on purpose, just because I thought I was going to get to dance all night. Why, it's only nine o'clock!

MASHA   Let's go on out and talk things over there. We'll decide about everything.

[*Sounds of "Good night!" "Good-bye!"* TUZENBACH *is heard laughing gaily.* EVERYONE *goes out.* ANFISA *and a* MAID *clear the table and put out the lights. The* NURSE *is heard singing.* ANDREI, *in a hat and overcoat, and* CHEBUTYKIN *come in.*]

CHEBUTYKIN   I never did manage to get married, because life's gone by me like lightning, and because I was crazy about your mother and she was married. . . .

ANDREI   People shouldn't get married. They shouldn't because it's boring.

CHEBUTYKIN   Maybe so, maybe so, but the loneliness! You can philosophize as much as you please, but loneliness is a terrible thing, Andrei boy. . . . Though on the other hand, really . . . of course, it doesn't make any difference one way or the other!

ANDREI   Let's hurry.

CHEBUTYKIN   What's the hurry? We'll make it.

ANDREI   I'm afraid my wife might stop me.

CHEBUTYKIN   Oh!

ANDREI   Tonight I won't play any myself, I'll just sit and watch. I don't feel very good. . . . Sometimes I feel as if I had asthma—what should I do for it, Ivan Romanich?

CHEBUTYKIN   Why ask me? *I* don't remember, Andrei boy. I don't know. . . .

ANDREI   Let's go out through the kitchen.

[THEY *go out. A ring, then another ring; voices and laughter.* IRINA *enters.*]

IRINA   What's that?

ANFISA (*Whispering*)   The carnival people! (*Another ring*)

IRINA   Nurse dear, tell them there isn't anyone at home. They'll have to excuse us.

[ANFISA *goes out.* IRINA *walks back and forth, lost in thought;* SHE *seems disturbed.* SOLYONY *comes in.*]

SOLYONY (*Perplexed*)   Nobody here. . . . Where is everybody?

IRINA   Gone home.

SOLYONY   That's funny. You're alone here?

IRINA   Alone. (*A pause*) Good-bye.

SOLYONY   A little while ago I lost control of myself, I wasn't tactful. But you are different from the rest of them, you are exalted, pure, you see the truth. . . . You are the only one there is that can understand me. I love you so, I'll love you to the end of—

IRINA   Good-bye. Go away.

SOLYONY   I can't live without you. (*Following her*) Oh, my ideal! (*Through his tears*) Oh, bliss! Those marvelous, glorious, incredible eyes—eyes like no other woman's I've ever seen. . . .

IRINA (*Coldly*)   Stop it, Vasili Vasilich!

SOLYONY   For the first time I'm speaking to you of love, and it's as if I were no longer on this earth, but on another planet. (HE *runs his hand across his forehead*) Well, it doesn't make any difference. I can't make you love me, of course. . . . But rivals, happy rivals—I can't stand those . . . can't stand them. I swear to you by all that is holy, I shall kill any rival. . . . Oh, wonderful one!

[NATASHA *comes in, a candle in her hand.* SHE *looks into one room, then into another, but walks by her* HUSBAND's *door without stopping.*]

NATASHA   There Andrei is. Let him read! Excuse me, Vasili Vasilich, I hadn't any idea you were in here. I'm not dressed.
SOLYONY   It doesn't make any difference to me. Good-bye!

[HE *goes out*]

NATASHA   And you're tired, dear—my poor little girl! (SHE *kisses* IRINA) If only you would go to bed a little earlier!
IRINA   Is Bobik asleep?
NATASHA   Asleep. But not sound asleep. By the way, dear, I keep meaning to speak to you about it, but either you're not home or else I haven't the time. . . . It seems to me that it's so cold and damp for Bobik in the nursery he has now. And your room is simply ideal for a child. My darling, my precious, do move in with Olga for a while!
IRINA (*Not understanding*)   Where?

[*A troika with bells is heard driving up to the house*]

NATASHA   You and Olga will be in one room, for the time being, and your room will be for Bobik. He's such a little dear, this morning I said to him, "Bobik, you're mine! Mine!" And he looked up at me with those darling

little eyes of his. (*A ring*) That must be Olga. How
late she is!

[A Maid *comes in and whispers in* Natasha's *ear*]

Natasha   Protopopov! What a funny man! Protopov's
here and wants me to go for a ride in his troika with him.
(*She laughs*) Men are so funny! (*A ring*) Someone else's
come. I suppose I might go, just for a few minutes.
(*To the* Maid) Tell him just a minute. . . . (*A ring*) There's
that doorbell again, it must be Olga.

[She *goes out*]

[*The* Maid *runs out;* Irina *sits thinking;* Kulygin
*and* Olga *enter,* Vershinin *just behind*]

Kulygin   Well, this is a fine state of affairs! And they
said they were going to have a party!
Vershinin   Strange. I left a little while ago, a half hour
ago, and they were expecting the carnival people.
Irina   They've all gone.
Kulygin   And Masha's gone too? Where's she gone?
And why's Protopopov waiting down there in his troika?
Who's he waiting for?
Irina   Don't ask questions. . . . I'm tired.
Kulygin   Little crosspatch!
Olga   The meeting lasted till just this minute. I'm ex-
hausted. Our headmistress is ill and I've had to take her
place. My head, how my head aches, my head . . . (She
*sits down*) Andrei lost two hundred rubles yesterday,
playing cards. Everybody in town is talking about it. . . .
Kulygin   Yes, and I got tired at the meeting, too.
Vershinin   My wife decided to give me a scare just

now, she almost poisoned herself. Everything's turned out
all right, and I certainly am glad—I can relax now. . . .
Then of course, we ought to leave? Well then, let me
wish you good-bye. Fyodor Ilich, come somewhere with
me! I can't go home tonight, I absolutely can't. . . .
Come on!

KULYGIN   I am tired. I'm not going. (HE *gets up*) I am
tired. Has my wife gone home?

IRINA   I suppose so.

KULYGIN (*Kissing* IRINA's *hand*)   Good-bye. Tomorrow
and the day after tomorrow I'm going to rest all day
long. Good-bye! (HE *goes*) I surely would like some tea.
I'd been counting on spending the evening in congenial
company and—O, *fallacem hominum spem!* Accusative
of exclamation. . . .

VERSHININ   It means I go by myself.

[HE *goes out with* KULYGIN, *whistling*]

OLGA   My head aches, my head . . . Andrei's lost—everybody in town's talking about it. . . . I'll go lie down.
(SHE *starts to go*) Tomorrow I'm free. . . . O my God,
what a relief that is! Tomorrow I'm free, the day after
tomorrow I'm free. . . . My head aches, my head . . .

[SHE *goes out*]

IRINA (*Alone*)   They've all gone. There's no one left.

[*An accordion is heard in the street, the* NURSE *is
singing in the next room*]

NATASHA (*Crossing the dining room in a fur coat and
cap, followed by a* MAID)   I'll be back in half an hour.
I'll only go for a short drive.

[SHE *goes out*]

IRINA (*Alone; yearningly*)   To Moscow! To Moscow!
To Moscow!

CURTAIN

# ACT III

OLGA'S AND IRINA'S ROOM. TO THE LEFT AND RIGHT *are beds, with screens around them. It is past two o'clock in the morning. Offstage a fire bell is being rung, for a fire that began a long time ago. No one in the house has gone to bed yet. MASHA is lying on the sofa, dressed as usual in a black dress. OLGA and ANFISA come in.*

ANFISA   They're down there now, just sitting by the stairs. I said, "Come upstairs. Please," I said, "you can't just sit here like this!"—they were crying. "Papa," they said, "we don't know where he is—" they said, "Maybe he's burned to death." What a thing to think of! And there're some people in the yard—they're not dressed either. . . .
OLGA (*Taking dresses from a wardrobe*)   Here, this gray one, take it . . . and this one here . . . the blouse, too. . . . And this skirt—take it, nurse dear. . . . My God, what a thing to happen—all Kirsanov Street's burned down, evidently. . . . Take this. . . . Take this. . . . (SHE *piles the clothes in* ANFISA'S *arms*) The Vershinins, poor things, certainly did get a fright. . . . Their house nearly burned down. They must spend the night here with us. . . . We can't send them home. . . . Poor Fedotik's had everything he owns burnt, there isn't a thing left. . . .

ANFISA  You'll have to call Ferapont, Olga darling, or
else I can't carry it. . . .
OLGA (*Ringing*)  Nobody answers. (SHE *calls through
the door*) Come here, whoever's down there. (*A window,
red with the glow of the fire, can be seen through the
open door; the fire department is heard going past the
house*) How terrible it all is! And how sick of it I am!

[FERAPONT *comes in*]

OLGA  Here, take these downstairs. . . . The Kelotilin
girls are down there by the staircase—give them to them.
Give them this, too. . . .
FERAPONT  Yes'm. In the year '12 Moscow burned too.
Good God Almighty! The Frenchmen were flabbergasted.
OLGA  Go on, get along. . . .
FERAPONT  Yes'm.

[HE *goes out*]

OLGA  Nurse darling, give it all away. We don't need
anything, give it all away, nurse. . . . I'm so tired I can
hardly stand on my feet. . . . We *can't* allow the Vershinins
to go home. The little girls can sleep in the living room,
and put Alexander Ignatich downstairs at the Baron's . . .
Fedotik at the Baron's, too, or else in our dining room.
. . . The Doctor's drunk, terribly drunk, just as if he'd
done it on purpose—we can't put anyone in with him.
And put Vershinin's wife in the living room too.
ANFISA (*Wearily*)  Olga darling, don't drive me away!
Don't drive me away!
OLGA  You're talking nonsense, nurse. Nobody's driving
you away.

*Irina and Tuzenbach*
Photograph by FRIEDMAN-ABELES

ANFISA (*Laying her head on* OLGA's *breast*)   My own,
treasure, I do the best I can, I do work. . . . I'm getting
weak, they'll all say, "Get out!" And where is there for
me to go? Where? Eighty years old . . . my eighty-
second year. . . .

OLGA   You sit down, nurse darling. . . . You're tired,
poor thing. . . . (SHE *gets her to sit down*) Rest, my
darling. How pale you look!

[NATASHA *enters*]

NATASHA   They're saying we ought to organize a com-
mittee right away to aid the victims of the fire. Well, why
not? It's a fine idea. After all, we ought to help the
poor, that's the duty of the rich. Bobik and Baby Sophie
are both sound asleep—sleeping as if nothing had happened!
. . . There're people here everywhere, wherever you go
the house is full of them. And there's all this flu in town
now, I'm so afraid the children may catch it.

OLGA (*Not listening to her*)   From this room you can't
see the fire, it's peaceful here. . . .

NATASHA   Uh-huh. . . . I must be a sight. (*In front of
the mirror*) They keep saying I've gained. . . . And it's
not so! It's not a bit so! And Masha's fast asleep—dead
tired, poor thing. . . . (*To* ANFISA, *coldly*) Don't you
dare sit down in my presence! Get up! Get out of here!
(ANFISA *goes out. A pause*) What you keep that old
woman for I simply do not understand!

OLGA (*Taken aback*)   I beg your pardon, I don't understand either. . . .

NATASHA   She's around here for no reason whatsoever.
She's a peasant, she ought to be in the country where she

belongs. . . . It's simply spoiling them! I like for everything in the house to have its proper place! There ought
not to be these useless people cluttering up the house.
(SHE *strokes* OLGA's *cheek*) Poor girl, you're tired. Our
headmistress is tired. When my little Sophie gets to be
a big girl and goes to the high school, I'm going to be
so afraid of you.

OLGA  I'm not going to be headmistress.

NATASHA  You're sure to be, Olga. It's already settled.

OLGA  I won't accept. I can't . . . I'm not strong enough.
. . . (SHE *drinks some water*) You were so rude to nurse
just now. Forgive me, I just haven't the strength to bear
it. . . . It's getting all black before my eyes. . . .

NATASHA (*Agitated*)  Forgive me, Olga, forgive me. . . .
I didn't mean to upset you.

[MASHA *gets up, takes her pillow, and goes out
angrily*]

OLGA  Try to understand, dear . . . perhaps we've been
brought up in an unusual way, but I can't bear this. This
sort of thing depresses me so, I get sick. . . . I just despair!

NATASHA  Forgive me, forgive me. (SHE *kisses her*)

OLGA  The least rudeness, even, an impolite word—it
upsets me. . . .

NATASHA  Sometimes I do say more than I should, that's
so, but you must admit, my dear, she *could* live in the
country.

OLGA  She's been with us thirty years already.

NATASHA  But now she just can't do anything, you know
that! Either I don't understand you or you don't want to
understand me. She's not fit for any work, she just
sleeps or sits.

OLGA   Well, let her sit.

NATASHA (*Surprised*)   What do you mean, let her sit?
Why, she's a servant. (*Tearfully*) I simply cannot understand you, Olga. I've got a nurse, a wet nurse, we've
got a maid, we've got a cook. . . . What do we have to
have that old woman for too? What *for*?

[*Behind the scene a fire alarm rings*]

OLGA   Tonight I have aged ten years.

NATASHA   We've got to settle things, Olga. You're at
the high school, I'm at home; you have the teaching,
and I have the housekeeping. And if I say something about
the servants, I know what I'm talking about: *I—know
—what—I'm—talking—about* . . . and tomorrow morning
that old thief, that old wretch (SHE *stamps her foot*),
that witch is going to be out of this house! Don't you
dare irritate me! Don't you dare! (*Collecting herself*)
Honestly, if you don't move downstairs we'll be quarreling
like this for the rest of our lives. This is awful!

[KULYGIN *comes in*]

KULYGIN   Where's Masha? It's time to go home. They
say the fire's dying down. (HE *stretches*) In spite of all
the wind, only one block's burned—at first it looked
as if the whole town would burn. (HE *sits down*) I am
exhausted, Olga my dear. . . . I often think if it hadn't
been Masha I'd have married you, Olga dear. You have
such a generous nature. . . . I am exhausted. (HE *listens
for something*)

OLGA   What is it?

KULYGIN   As if he'd done it on purpose, the Doctor's got
drunk, he's terribly drunk. As if he'd done it on purpose!

(He *gets up*) I do believe he's coming up here. . . .
Hear him? Yes, up here. . . . (He *laughs*) If he isn't the
. . . I'll hide. (He *goes to the wardrobe and stands between
it and the wall*) What a rascal!

OLGA   For two years he doesn't drink, and now all of
a sudden he goes and gets drunk. . . .

[She *follows* Natasha *to the back of the room.*

Chebutykin *enters; without staggering, like a sober
person,* He *crosses the room, stops, looks around, then
goes to the washbasin and begins to wash his hands.*]

CHEBUTYKIN (*Gloomily*)   The devil take every one of
them . . . every one of them. . . . They think I'm a
doctor, know how to treat anything there is, and I don't
know a thing, I've forgotten everything I ever did know,
I remember nothing, absolutely nothing.

[OLGA *and* NATASHA *leave the room without his
noticing*]

CHEBUTYKIN   The devil take them. Last Wednesday I
treated a woman at Zasyp—dead, and it's my fault she's
dead. Yes. . . . Twenty-five years ago I used to know a
little something, but now I don't remember a thing. One
single thing. Maybe I'm not a man at all, but just look
like one—maybe it just looks like I've got arms and legs
and a head. Maybe I don't even exist, and it only looks like
I walk and eat and sleep. (He *cries*) Oh, if only I didn't
exist! (He *stops crying; gloomily*) The devil only knows.
. . . Day before yesterday they were talking at the club;
they talked about Shakespeare, Voltaire. . . . I haven't
read them, I never have read them at all, but I looked
like I'd read them. And the others did too, the same as me.

So cheap! So low! And that woman I killed Wednesday—
she came back to me, and it all came back to me, and
everything inside me felt all twisted, all vile, all nauseating.
. . . I went and got drunk. . . .

[IRINA, VERSHININ, *and* TUZENBACH *come in;* TUZEN-
BACH *is wearing new and stylish civilian clothes*]

IRINA  Let's sit in here. Nobody will be coming in here.
VERSHININ  If it hadn't been for the soldiers the whole
town would have burnt up. Brave men, those! (HE *rubs
his hands with pleasure*) The salt of the earth! Ah,
those are first-rate men!
KULYGIN (*Going up to them*)  What's the time, gentle-
men?
TUZENBACH  Going on four. It's getting light.
IRINA  They're all sitting there in the dining room, nobody
thinks of leaving, and that Solyony of yours sits there.
. . . (*To* CHEBUTYKIN) Oughtn't you to go to bed,
Doctor?
CHEBUTYKIN  Doesn't matter. . . . Thank you. . . . (HE
*combs his beard*)
KULYGIN (*Laughing*)  You're tight, Ivan Romanich!
(HE *slaps him on the back*) Bravo! *In vino veritas*, as
the ancients used to say.
TUZENBACH  Everybody keeps asking me to get up a
concert to help the people whose houses burned.
IRINA  Yes, but who's there to . . . ?
TUZENBACH  We could arrange one if we wanted to.
Marya Sergeevna, in my opinion, is a wonderful pianist.
KULYGIN  Yes indeed, wonderful.
IRINA  She's forgotten how, by now. She hasn't played
for three years—four.

TUZENBACH  Here in this town there is not a soul who
understands music, not a single soul; but I, I do understand
it, and I give you my word of honor that Marya
Sergeevna plays magnificently, almost with genius.

KULYGIN  You're right, Baron. I love her very much,
Masha. She's wonderful.

TUZENBACH  To be able to play so beautifully and all the
time to know that no one, no one, understands you!

KULYGIN  (*Sighing*)  Yes. . . . But would it be proper
for her to appear in a public concert? (*A pause*) Really,
gentlemen, I know nothing about it. Perhaps it would be
quite all right. You have to admit that our principal
is a fine man, in fact a very fine man, very intelligent,
too; but his views *are* a little . . . Of course, it isn't any of
his affair, but just the same, if you think I ought to, I'll
speak to him about it.

[CHEBUTYKIN *picks up a porcelain clock and examines it*]

VERSHININ  I got all covered with dirt at the fire—I
look pretty disreputable. (*A pause*) Yesterday just by
accident I heard someone say that they may be sending
our brigade a long way off—some of them said to Poland,
some of them said to Siberia, to Chita.

TUZENBACH  I heard that too. Well, what is there you
can do? The town will be completely empty.

IRINA  And we'll leave too!

CHEBUTYKIN  (*Drops the clock, smashing it*)  To
smithereens!

[*A pause; everyone looks embarrassed and upset*]

KULYGIN  (*Picking up the pieces*)  To break such an
expensive thing—oh, Ivan Romanich, Ivan Romanich!
You get a zero-minus in deportment!

IRINA   That's Mother's clock.

CHEBUTYKIN   Maybe. . . . If it's Mother's, then it's Mother's. Maybe I didn't break it but it only looks like I broke it. Maybe it only looks like we exist, and really we don't. I don't know anything, nobody knows anything. (*At the door*) What are you staring at? Natasha's having an affair with Protopopov, and you don't see that. You sit there and see nothing, and Natasha's having an affair with Protopopov. . . . (*Singing*) "Tell me how you like this little present!"

[HE *goes out*]

VERSHININ   Yes. . . . (HE *laughs*) How strange all this is, in reality! When the fire started I rushed home; I got there, looked around . . . the house was safe and sound, not in any danger at all, but there my two little girls were, standing in the doorway in just their underwear, their mother gone, people rushing around, horses running by, dogs, and my little girls' faces were so anxious and terrified and beseeching and—I don't know what; it wrung my heart to look at those faces. My God, I thought, what these girls still have to go through in the rest of their lives, in all the years to come! I picked them up and ran, and I kept thinking one thing: what they still have to live through in this world! (*Fire alarm; a pause*) I got here and here was their mother—she was shouting, she got angry.

[MASHA *comes in with the pillow and sits down on the sofa*]

VERSHININ   And while my little girls were standing in the doorway in just their underwear, and the street was red with the fire, the noise was terrible, I started thinking that it's almost what happened long ago, when the enemy attacked unexpectedly, looting and burning. . . . And yet, in reality, what a difference there is between what things are now and what they were then! And when a little more time has passed, two or three hundred years, people will look in horror and mockery at this life we live now, and everything we do now will seem to them clumsy, and difficult, and terribly uncomfortable and strange. Oh, what life will be like then! What life will be like then! (HE *laughs*) Sorry, I've started philosophizing again. But do let me go on, ladies and gentlemen. I feel terribly like philosophizing, I'm in just the right frame of mind. (*A pause*) Looks like they're all asleep. So I say: What life will be like then! Can you imagine! Here in this town there are only three of your kind now, but in the generations to come there will be more and more and more; the time will come when everything will get to be the way you want it to be, everybody will live like you, and then after a while you yourselves will be out-of-date, there'll be people born who'll be better than you. . . . (HE *laughs*) I'm in a most peculiar frame of mind tonight. I want like the devil to live. (HE *sings*) "Unto love all ages bow, its pangs are blest . . ."

MASHA    Da-da-dum . . .

VERSHININ    Da-dum . . .

MASHA    Da-da-da?

VERSHININ    Da-da-da! (HE *laughs*)

[FEDOTIK *comes in*]

FEDOTIK (*Dancing*)    Burnt to ashes! Burnt to ashes! Everything I had in this world! (*Laughter*)

IRINA   What kind of joke is that? Is it really all burnt?

FEDOTIK (*Laughing*)   Every single last thing! There's not one thing left! The guitar's burnt, and the camera burnt, and all my letters are burnt. . . . And I meant to give you a little notebook, and it's burnt too. . . .

[SOLYONY *enters*]

IRINA   No, please go away, Vasili Vasilich. You can't come in here.

SOLYONY   But why is it the Baron can and I can't?

VERSHININ   We ought to be going, really. How's the fire?

SOLYONY   They say it's dying down. No, it's a very strange thing to me, why is it the Baron can and I can't? (HE *takes out a bottle of perfume and sprinkles it on himself*)

VERSHININ   Da-da-dum?

MASHA   Da-dum!

VERSHININ (*Laughing, to* SOLYONY)   Let's go on in the dining room.

SOLYONY   All right, but there'll be a note made of this. "This moral could be made more clear. But 'twould annoy the geese, I fear." (HE looks at TUZENBACH) *He-ere*, chicky, chicky, chicky!

[HE *goes out with* VERSHININ *and* FEDOTIK]

IRINA   That Solyony! There's smoke all over everything. . . . (*In surprise*) The Baron's asleep! Baron! Baron!

TUZENBACH (*Waking up*)   I'm tired, only I . . . the brickyard . . . I'm not delirious, I really am going to start work there soon. . . . I've already talked it over with them. (*To* IRINA, *tenderly*) You're so pale and beautiful and enchanting. . . . It seems to me your paleness brightens

the dark air like light . . . You're sad, you're dissatisfied
with life. . . . Oh, come away with me, let's go and work
together!

MASHA   Nikolai Lvovich, go away from here!

TUZENBACH (*Laughing*) You're here? I didn't see you.
(HE *kisses* IRINA's *hand*) Good-bye, I'm going. I look
at you now, and it reminds me of how long ago on your
birthday you were so happy and cheerful, and talked
about the joy of work. . . . And what a happy life I saw
before me then! Where is it? (HE *kisses her hand*) You
have tears in your eyes. Go to bed, it's already getting
light. . . . It's beginning to be morning. . . . If only I
might give my life for you!

MASHA   Nikolai Lvovich, go away! Why, really, what . . .

TUZENBACH   I'm going.

[HE *goes out*]

MASHA (*Lying down*)   Are you asleep, Fyodor?

KULYGIN   What?

MASHA   You should go home.

KULYGIN   My darling Masha, my precious Masha . . .

IRINA   She's worn out. . . . Let her rest, Fyodor dear.

KULYGIN   I'll go in just a minute. My good, wonderful
wife . . . I love you, my only one. . . .

MASHA (*Angrily*)   *Amo, amas, amat, amamus, amatis,
amant.*

KULYGIN (*Laughing*)   No, really, she's amazing. I've
been married to you for seven years, and it seems as if we
were married only yesterday. Word of honor! No, really,
you're an amazing woman. I am satisfied, I am satisfied,
I am satisfied!

MASHA    Bored, bored, bored! ... (SHE *sits up*) I can't
get it out of my head. It's simply revolting. It sticks in
my head like a nail, I can't keep quiet about it any longer.
I mean about Andrei . . . he's mortgaged this house at
the bank and his wife's got hold of all the money. But
the house doesn't belong just to him, it belongs to the four
of us! He ought to know that if he's a decent man.
KULYGIN    Must you, MASHA? What's it to you? Poor
Andrei's in debt to everybody—well, God help him!
MASHA    Just the same, it's revolting. (SHE *lies down*)
KULYGIN    You and I aren't poor. I work, I go to the
high school, I give lessons afterwards. . . . I'm an honest
man . . . a simple man. . . . *Omnia mea mecum porto*,
as the saying goes.
MASHA    I don't need anything, but the injustice of it
nauseates me. (*A pause*) Go on, Fyodor.
KULYGIN (*Kissing her*)    You're tired, rest for half an hour,
and I'll sit there and wait. . . . Sleep. . . . (HE *starts to
leave*) I am satisfied, I am satisfied, I am satisfied.

   [HE *goes out*]

IRINA    No, really, how petty our Andrei's become, how
lifeless and old he's got, at the side of that woman! Once
he was preparing to be a professor, a scholar, and yesterday
he was boasting that he's finally managed to get made
a member of the county board. He a member, Protopopov
chairman. . . . Everybody in town is talking about it,
laughing at it, and he's the only one that knows nothing,
that sees nothing. . . . And now everybody's run off to
the fire, and he sits there in his room and doesn't pay
any attention to anything, he just plays the violin.

(*Nervously*) Oh, it's awful, awful, awful! (SHE *cries*)
I can't stand any more, I can't stand it! . . . I can't, I
can't. . . .

[OLGA *comes in and begins to straighten her dressing
table*]

IRINA (*Sobbing loudly*)   Throw me out, throw me out,
I can't stand any more!
OLGA (*Alarmed*)   What is it, what is it? Darling!
IRINA (*Sobbing*)   Where? Where's it all gone? Where
is it? Oh, my God, my God! I've forgotten everything,
forgotten . . . it's all mixed up in my head, I don't remember what *window* is in Italian, or—or *ceiling*. . . . I'm
forgetting everything, every day I forget, and life goes
by and won't ever come back, won't ever, we'll never
go to Moscow, we won't ever . . . now I see that we
won't ever . . .
OLGA   Darling, darling . . .
IRINA (*Trying to control herself*)   Oh, I'm miserable . . .
I can't work, I'm not ever going to work. That's enough,
that's enough! First I worked at the telegraph office,
now I work at the county board, and I hate and despise
every last thing they have me do. . . . I'm already almost
twenty-four, I've been working for years and years
already, my brain is drying up, I'm getting thin, getting
ugly, getting old, and there's nothing, nothing—there isn't
the least satisfaction of any kind—and the years are
going by, and every day, over and over, everything's
getting farther away from any real life, beautiful life,
everything's going farther and farther into some abyss. . . .
I am in despair, I can't understand how I'm alive, how
I haven't killed myself long ago. . . .

OLGA   Don't cry, my own little girl, don't cry. . . .
I suffer, too.
IRINA   I'm not crying, I'm not crying. . . . That's enough.
. . . See, now I'm not crying any more. . . . That's
enough, that's enough!
OLGA   Darling, I tell you as your sister, as your friend:
If you want my advice, marry the Baron!

[IRINA *weeps silently*]

OLGA   You know you respect him, you think so much
of him. . . . He's ugly, it's true, but he's such an honest
man, such a good man. . . . You know, people don't marry
for love, but for duty. At least, I think so, and I would
marry without being in love. If someone proposed to
me, no matter who it was, I'd marry him, as long as he
was a decent man. I'd marry an old man, even. . . .

IRINA   I was always waiting till we moved to Moscow,
I'd meet the real one there—I used to dream about him,
love him. . . . But it's all turned out nonsense, all nonsense!
OLGA (*Embracing her* SISTER)   My dear, beautiful sister,
I understand it all: When Baron Nikolai Lvovich left
the army and came to see us in his civilian clothes, he
looked so homely to me I absolutely started to cry. . . . He
said, "Why are you crying?" How could I tell him!
But if it were God's will he should marry you, I'd be happy.
That would be different, you know, completely different.

[NATASHA, *with a candle, comes out of the door on
the right, crosses the stage, and goes out through the
door on the left, without speaking*]

MASHA (*Sitting up*)   She walks like the one that started
the fire.

OLGA  Masha, you're silly. The silliest one in the whole family—that's you. Please forgive me. (*A pause*)

MASHA  I want to confess, dear sisters. Inside I—I can't keep on this way any longer. I'll confess to you and then never again to anybody, never again. . . . In a minute I'll say it. (*In a low voice*) It's my secret, but you ought to know it. . . . I can't keep quiet any longer. . . . (*A pause*) I love, love . . . I love that man. . . . The one you just saw. . . . Oh, why not say it? In one word, I love Vershinin.

OLGA (*Going behind her screen*)  Stop it. Anyway, I don't hear you.

MASHA  What is there I can do? (SHE *holds her head in her hands*) At first he seemed strange to me, then I felt sorry for him . . . then I fell in love with him, fell in love with his voice, his words, his misfortunes, his two little girls. . . .

OLGA (*Behind the screen*)  Anyway, I don't hear you. Whatever silly things you're saying, anyway, I don't hear you.

MASHA  Oh, you're so silly, Olga. I love him—it means, it's my fate. It means, it's my lot. . . . And he loves me. . . . It's all so strange. Yes? It isn't good? (SHE *takes* IRINA *by the hand and draws her close to her*) Oh my darling, how are we going to live our lives, what is going to become of us? When you read some novel then it all seems so old and so easy to understand, but when you're in love yourself you see that no one knows anything, and everyone has to decide for himself. . . . My darlings, my sisters, I've confessed to you, now I'll be silent. . . . From now on I'll be like Gogol's madman . . . silence . . . silence . . .

[ANDREI *comes in, followed by* FERAPONT]

ANDREI (*Angrily*) What is it you want? I don't understand.

FERAPONT (*Standing in the doorway, impatiently*) Andrei Sergeevich, I've told you ten times already.

ANDREI In the first place, to you I am not Andrei Sergeevich, but your honor!

FERAPONT The firemen, your honor, want to know if you'll please let them go to the river through your garden. Because the way it is they have to go around and around, they're getting all worn out.

ANDREI All right. Tell them all right.

[FERAPONT *leaves*]

ANDREI What a bore! . . . Where's Olga? (OLGA *comes out from behind the screen*) I've come to get the key to the cupboard from you, I've lost mine. You've got one of those little keys. . . . [OLGA *hands him the key, without speaking.* IRINA *goes behind her screen. A pause.*) What a tremendous fire! It's started to die down now. . . . The devil, that Ferapont made me lose my temper—that was stupid to say that. . . . Your honor. . . . (*A pause*) Why don't you say something, Olga? (*A pause*) It's about time you stopped this silliness . . . pouting like this without rhyme or reason. . . . Masha, you're here, Irina's here, well, that's just fine—let's get things settled once and for all. What is it you've got against me? What is it?

OLGA Let it go now, Andrei dear. We'll straighten things out tomorrow. (*In an agitated voice*) What a dreadful night!

ANDREI (*In great confusion and embarrassment*) Don't

get all upset. I'm asking you perfectly calmly: What is
it you've got against me? Come right out with it.
VERSHININ'S VOICE (*Offstage*)   Da-da-dum!
MASHA (*In a loud voice, getting up*)   Da-da-dah! (*To*
OLGA) Good-bye Olga, God bless you! (SHE *goes behind
the screen and kisses* IRINA) Have a good sleep. . . .
Good-bye, Andrei. Leave them alone now, they're worn
out. . . . Tomorrow we can straighten things out.

   [SHE *goes out*]

OLGA   That's right, Andrei dear, let's put it off until
tomorrow. . . . (SHE *goes behind the screen on her side
of the room*) It's time to go to sleep.
ANDREI   I'll only say this much and go. Right away. . . .
In the first place, you've got something against Natasha,
my wife, and I've seen that from the very first day we
were married. Natasha is a splendid, honest person, straight-
forward and sincere—that is my opinion. I love and
respect my wife—respect her, you understand, and I
demand that others respect her too. I repeat, she's an honest,
sincere person, and anything you've got against her, if I
may say so, is just your imagination. . . . (*A pause*) In
the second place, you seem to be angry with me because
I'm not a professor, don't in some way advance knowledge.
But I am in the service of the government, I am a member
of the county board, and this service of mine is to me just
as sacred and lofty as the service of knowledge. I am a
member of the county board and I am proud of it, if
you want to know. . . . (*A pause*) In the third place. . . .
I have something else to say. . . . I've mortgaged the house
without your permission. . . . For that I am to blame,
I admit it, and I beg you to forgive me. My debts forced

me to. . . . Thirty-five thousand. . . . I no longer play cards, gave them up long ago, but the main thing I can say to justify myself is this, that you—that you're girls, you get a pension, I, though, didn't get . . . earnings, so to speak. . . . (*A pause*)

KULYGIN (*At the door*)   Isn't Masha here? (*Anxiously*) But where is she? This is strange. . . .

[HE *goes out*]

ANDREI   They won't listen. Natasha's a splendid, honest person. (HE *walks up and down silently, then stops*) When I got married I thought we'd be happy . . . all of us happy . . . but my God! . . . (HE *cries*) My dearest sisters, darling sisters, don't believe me, don't believe . . .

[HE *goes out*]

KULYGIN (*at the door anxiously*)   Where's Masha? Isn't Masha here? What an extraordinary thing!

[HE *goes out*]

[*Fire alarm; the stage is empty*]

IRINA (*Behind the screen*)   Olga! Who's that knocking on the floor?

OLGA   It's the Doctor, it's Ivan Romanich. He's drunk.

IRINA   What a miserable night! (*A pause*) Olga! (SHE *looks out from behind the screen*) Did you hear? They're taking the brigade away from us, sending it way off somewhere.

OLGA   It's only a rumor.

IRINA   Then we'll be left all alone. . . . Olga!

OLGA   Well?

IRINA   Dearest sister, darling sister, I respect the Baron,

I admire the Baron, he's a marvelous person, I'll marry him, I agree, only let's go to Moscow! Let's go, oh please let's go! There's nothing in this world better than Moscow! Let's go, Olga! Let's go!

CURTAIN

# ACT IV

---

THE OLD GARDEN OF THE PROZOROVS' HOUSE. AT THE
*end of a long avenue of fir trees there is the river. On
the other bank of the river is a forest. To the right of the
house there is a terrace. Here on a table there are
bottles and glasses; it is evident that they have just been
drinking champagne. Occasionally people from the
street cut through the garden to get to the river; five
or six soldiers go through, walking fast.* CHEBUTYKIN,
*in a genial mood which does not leave him during the
act, is sitting in an easy chair in the garden;* HE *wears his
uniform cap and is holding a walking stick.* IRINA,
KULYGIN *with a decoration around his neck and with
no moustache, and* TUZENBACH *are standing on the
terrace saying good-bye to* FEDOTIK *and* RODE, *who are
coming down the steps; both officers are in parade
uniform.*

TUZENBACH (*Embracing* FEDOTIK) You're a fine man,
we got along so well together. (HE *embraces* RODE)
One more time. . . . Good-bye, old man. . . .
IRINA *Au revoir!*
FEDOTIK It isn't *au revoir*, it's good-bye; we'll never see
each other again!
KULYGIN Who knows? (HE *wipes his eyes and smiles*)

Here I've started crying.

IRINA   Some day or other we'll meet again.

FEDOTIK   In ten years—fifteen? By then we'll hardly recognize each other, we'll say "How do you do" coldly. . . . (HE *takes a photograph*) Stand still. . . . One more time, it's the last time.

RODE (*Embracing* TUZENBACH)   We'll never see each other again. . . . (HE *kisses* IRINA's *hand*) Thank you for everything, for everything!

FEDOTIK (*Annoyed*)   Oh, stand still!

TUZENBACH   Please God, we'll see each other again. Write us now. Be sure to write us.

RODE (*Looking around the garden*)   Good-bye, trees! (HE *shouts*) Yoo-hoo! (*A pause*) Good-bye, echo!

KULYGIN   With any luck you'll get married there in Poland. . . . Your Polish wife will hug you and call you *kochany*! (HE *laughs*)

FEDOTIK (*Looking at his watch*)   We've less than an hour left. Solyony's the only one from our battery that's going on the barge, the rest of us are going with the enlisted men. Three batteries are leaving today, three more to-morrow—and then peace and quiet will descend on the town.

TUZENBACH   And awful boredom.

RODE   But where's Marya Sergeevna?

KULYGIN   Masha's in the garden.

FEDOTIK   We must say good-bye to her.

RODE   Good-bye. We must go, otherwise I'll start crying. (HE *hurriedly embraces* TUZENBACH *and* KULYGIN, *and kisses* IRINA's *hand*) It was so nice living here.

FEDOTIK (*To* KULYGIN)   This is for you to remember

us by . . . a notebook with a pencil. . . . We'll go on
down to the river this way. . . .

[They *go off, both looking back*]

Rode (*Shouting*)   Yoo-hoo!
Fedotik (*Shouting*)   Good-bye!

[*At the back of the stage* Fedotik *and* Rode *meet*
Masha *and say good-bye to her;* She *goes off with them*]

Irina   They're gone. . . .

[She *sits down on the bottom step of the terrace*]

Chebutykin   And forgot to say good-bye to me.
Irina   And what about you?
Chebutykin   Well, I forgot, somehow. Anyway, I'll
be seeing them again soon, I'm leaving tomorrow.
Yes. . . . Only one more day. In a year more they'll retire
me, I'll come back again and live out the rest of my days
near you. . . . Only one more year and I get my pen-
sion. . . . (He *puts a newspaper in his pocket, takes a
newspaper out of his pocket*) I'll come back here to you
and lead a completely new life. I'll get to be such a sober,
Gu-Gu-God-fearing, respectable man.
Irina   Yes, you really ought to, my dove. Somehow or
other you ought.
Chebutykin   Yes. I feel so. (He *begins to sing softly*)
Ta-ra-ra-boom-de-aye . . . / Sit on a log I may . . .
Kulygin   You're incorrigible, Ivan Romanich! You're
incorrigible!
Chebutykin   Yes, if only I had *you* for a teacher!
Then I'd reform.

IRINA  Fyodor's shaved off his moustache. I can't bear to look at him.

KULYGIN  And what of it?

CHEBUTYKIN  I could say what that face of yours looks like now—but I don't dare.

KULYGIN  Well, what of it? It's the accepted thing, it's the *modus vivendi*. . . . Our principal's shaved off his moustache, so when they made me the assistant principal I shaved mine off too. Nobody likes it, but it doesn't make any difference to me. I am satisfied. With a moustache or without a moustache, I am satisfied. . . .

[HE *sits down.*

ANDREI *walks across the back of the stage, wheeling a baby carriage with the baby asleep in it.*]

IRINA  Ivan Romanich, my dove, my darling, I'm terribly worried. You were on the boulevard yesterday, tell me, what happened there?

CHEBUTYKIN  What happened? Nothing. Piffle! (HE *reads the newspaper*) What's the difference!

KULYGIN  What they say is that Solyony and the Baron met each other yesterday on the boulevard, up by the theater—

TUZENBACH  Stop it! Why, really, what . . .

[HE *waves his hand and goes into the house*]

KULYGIN  Up by the theater . . . Solyony started bothering the Baron, and the Baron wouldn't stand for it, he said something insulting . . .

CHEBUTYKIN  I don't know. It's all nonsense.

KULYGIN  There was a teacher in some seminary that wrote *Nonsense*! on a theme, and the pupil thought it

was *Nonesuch!*—thought it was Latin. (HE *laughs*)
Amazingly funny! They say it looks like Solyony's in love
with Irina, and he hates the Baron. . . . That's understandable. Irina is a very nice girl. She's quite like Masha,
even—always thinking about something. Only you have
a milder disposition, Irina. Though as a matter of fact
Masha has a fine disposition too. I love her, Masha.

[*At the rear of the garden, behind the stage, someone
shouts: "Yoo-hoo!"*]

IRINA (*Shivering*) Somehow everything frightens me
today. (*A pause*) I've got everything packed already,
I'm sending my things off right after dinner. The Baron
and I are getting married tomorrow, tomorrow we leave
for the brickyard, and day after tomorrow I'll already be
at school, the new life will have begun. Somehow God
will help me! When I passed my teacher's examination
I wept for joy . . . so grateful . . . (*A pause*) In a little
the horse and the cart will be here for my things. . . .

KULYGIN That's all right, only somehow it isn't
serious. It's all just ideas, and hardly anything really
serious. Still, though, I wish you luck from the bottom
of my heart.

CHEBUTYKIN (*With emotion*) My dearest, my treasure.
. . . My wonderful girl. . . . You have gone on far ahead,
I'll never catch up with you. I'm left behind like a bird
that's grown old, too old to fly. Fly on, my dears, fly on
and God be with you! (*A pause*) It's a shame you shaved
off your moustache, Fyodor Ilich.

KULYGIN That's enough from you! (HE *sighs*) Well,
the soldiers leave today, and then everything will be the
way it used to be. No matter what they say, Masha is a

good, honest woman, I love her very much, and I'm
thankful for my fate. . . . People have such different fates.
. . . There's a man named Kozyrev that works in the tax
department here. He went to school with me, but they
expelled him from high school because he just couldn't
manage to understand *ut consecutivum*. Now he's terribly
poor, sick, and when we meet each other I say to him,
"Hello, *ut consecutivum!*" Yes, he says, that's it, *consecutivum*, and he coughs. . . . And I've been lucky all my life,
I've even got the Order of Stanislav Second Class, I
myself am teaching others, now, that *ut consecutivum*.
Of course, I'm an intelligent man, more intelligent than lots
of people, but happiness doesn't consist in that. . . .

[*Inside the house someone plays "The Maiden's Prayer"
on the piano*]

IRINA   Tomorrow evening I won't be hearing that
"Maiden's Prayer" any more, I won't be meeting that
Protopopov. . . . (*A pause*) And Protopopov's sitting there
in the living room—he's come today too. . . .
KULYGIN   The headmistress still hasn't arrived?
IRINA   No. They've sent for her. If only you knew how
hard it is for me to live here alone, without Olga. . . .
She lives at the high school; she's the headmistress, all
day she's busy with her job, and I'm alone, I'm bored,
there's nothing to do, I hate the very room I live in. . . .
So I just made up my mind: If it's fated for me not to
live in Moscow, then that's that. It means, it's fate.
There's nothing to be done about it. . . . It's all in God's
hands, that's the truth. Nikolai Lvovich proposed to me.
. . . Well? I thought it over and made up my mind.
He's a good man, it really is extraordinary how good . . .

and all at once it was as if my soul had wings, I was happy, I felt all relieved, I wanted to work all over again, to work! . . . Only something happened yesterday, there's something mysterious hanging over me. . . .

CHEBUTYKIN   Nonesuch. Nonsense.

NATASHA (*At the window*)   The headmistress!

KULYGIN   The headmistress has arrived. Let's go on in.

[HE *and* IRINA *go into the house*]

CHEBUTYKIN (*Reading the newspaper and singing softly to himself*)   Ta-ra-ra-boom-de-aye . . . / Sit on a log I may . . .

[MASHA *comes up;* ANDREI *passes across the back of the stage wheeling the baby carriage*]

MASHA   He sits there. There he sits. . . .

CHEBUTYKIN   So what?

MASHA (*Sitting down*)   Nothing. . . . (*A pause*) Did you love my mother?

CHEBUTYKIN   Very much.

MASHA   And she loved you?

CHEBUTYKIN (*After a pause*)   I don't remember any more.

MASHA   Is my man here? That's the way our cook Marfa used to talk about her policeman—my man. Is my man here?

CHEBUTYKIN   Not yet.

MASHA   When you get happiness in snatches, in shreds, and then lose it the way I'm losing it, little by little you get coarse, you get furious. (SHE *points to her breast*) In here I'm boiling. . . . (SHE *looks at* ANDREI, *who again crosses the stage with the baby carriage*) There's that little brother of ours, our Andrei. . . . All our hopes vanished. Once upon a time there was a great bell, thousands

of people were raising it, ever so much work and money
had gone into it, and all of a sudden it fell and broke.
All of a sudden, for no reason at all. And that's Andrei. . . .

ANDREI   Aren't they ever going to quiet down in the
house? What a hubbub!

CHEBUTYKIN   In a little. (HE *looks at his watch*) I've
got an old-fashioned watch, it strikes. . . . (HE *winds
the watch, it strikes*) The first and the second and the fifth
batteries leave at one o'clock sharp. (*A pause*) And I
leave tomorrow.

MASHA   For good?

CHEBUTYKIN   I don't know. Maybe I'll be back in a
year. Except . . . the devil knows. . . . What's the difference! . . .

   [*Somewhere in the distance a harp and violin are
   playing*]

ANDREI   The town will be deserted. It will be as if they'd
put all the lights out. (*A pause*) Something happened
yesterday up by the theater—everybody's talking about
it, but I haven't any idea.

CHEBUTYKIN   Nothing. Just nonsense. Solyony started
bothering the Baron, and he got mad and insulted him, and
finally Solyony had to challenge him to a duel. (HE
*looks at his watch*) It's already about time. . . . At half
past twelve, in the state forest over there, the one you can
see across the river. . . . Piff-Paff! (HE *laughs*) Solyony's
got the idea he's Lermontov, and even writes little poems.
A joke is a joke, but this is his third duel already.

MASHA   Whose?

CHEBUTYKIN   Solyony's.

MASHA   And the Baron?

CHEBUTYKIN What about the Baron? (*A pause*)

MASHA It's all mixed up in my head. . . . Just the same, I say it isn't right to allow them to. He might wound the Baron or even kill him.

CHEBUTYKIN The Baron's a good man, but one baron more, one baron less—what's the difference?

[*Someone shouts from beyond the garden: "Yoo-hoo!"*]

You wait. That's Skvortsov shouting, one of the seconds. He's in the boat. (*A pause*)

ANDREI In my opinion, to take part in a duel, to be present at one even in the capacity of a doctor, is simply immoral.

CHEBUTYKIN It only looks that way. . . . We're not here, there's nothing in this world, we don't exist, it looks like we exist. . . . And what's the difference anyway!

MASHA That's how it is—the whole day long they talk, talk. . . . (SHE *walks away*) To live in a climate where you have to expect it to snow every minute—and then on top of it, that's the way they talk. (SHE *stops*) I won't go into that house, I can't bear it. . . . Tell me when Vershinin comes. . . . (SHE *goes off along the avenue of trees*) And the birds are flying south already. . . . Swans or geese. . . . (SHE *looks up*) My beautiful ones, my happy ones. . . .

[SHE *goes out*]

ANDREI Our house will be deserted. The officers are leaving, you're leaving, my sister's getting married, and I'll be the only one left.

CHEBUTYKIN And your wife?

[FERAPONT *comes in with some papers*]

ANDREI   A wife's a wife. She's honest, sincere—well, kind, but at the same time there's something in her that makes her a kind of blind, petty, hairy animal. In any case, she's not a human being. I'm saying this to you as my friend, the only one I can really talk to. I love Natasha, that's so, but sometimes she seems to me astonishingly vulgar, and then I just despair, I can't understand why I love her as much as I do—or anyway, did. . . .

CHEBUTYKIN (*Getting up*)   Brother, I'm going away tomorrow, we may never see each other again, so here's my advice to you. Put on your hat, take your walking stick in your hand, and get out . . . get out, keep going, don't ever look back. And the farther you go the better.

> [SOLYONY *walks across the back of the stage, along with two* OFFICERS; *seeing* CHEBUTYKIN, HE *turns toward him—the other* OFFICERS *walk on*]

SOLYONY   Doctor, it's time! It's already half past twelve. (HE *shakes hands with* ANDREI)

CHEBUTYKIN   In a minute. I'm sick of all of you. (To ANDREI) If anybody wants me, Andrei boy, tell them I'll be back in a minute. . . . (HE *sighs*) Oh—oh—oh!

SOLYONY   Before he'd time to get his breath / The bear was hugging him to death. (HE *goes with him*) What are you groaning about, old man?

CHEBUTYKIN   Well . . .

SOLYONY   How're you feeling?

CHEBUTYKIN (*Angrily*)   As snug as a bug in a rug!

SOLYONY   The old man's unduly excited. I'm only going to indulge myself a little, I'll just shoot him like a snipe. (HE *takes out a bottle of perfume and sprinkles it on his hands*) I've used up the whole bottle today, and they

still smell. They smell like a corpse. (*A pause*) So. . . .
Remember the poem? "But he, the rebel, seeks the storm /
As if in tempests there were peace . . ."
CHEBUTYKIN  Uh-huh. "Before he'd time to get his breath
The bear was hugging him to death."

[HE *and* SOLYONY *go out.*

PEOPLE *shout,* "*Yoo-hoo! Yoo-hoo!*" ANDREI *and*
FERAPONT *come in.*]

FERAPONT  Papers to sign. . . .
ANDREI (*Nervously*)  Leave me alone! Leave me alone!
*I beg you!*

[HE *goes off with the carriage*]

FERAPONT  But that's what papers are for, you know,
to sign.

[HE *goes to the back of the stage.*

IRINA *and* TUZENBACH *come in;* HE *is wearing a straw hat.*
KULYGIN *crosses the stage, calling:* "*Yoo-hoo, Masha!*
*Yoo-hoo!*"]

TUZENBACH  I believe he's the only person in town that's
glad the soldiers are leaving.
IRINA  That's understandable. (*A pause*) The town's
getting all empty.
TUZENBACH (*After looking at his watch*)  Dear, I'll be
back in a minute.
IRINA  Where are you going?
TUZENBACH  I have to go in to town, to—to say good-
bye to my friends.
IRINA  That's not so. . . . Nikolai, why are you so upset
today? (*A pause*) What happened yesterday, by the
theater?

TUZENBACH (*With a movement of impatience*) In an hour I'll come back and be with you again. (HE *kisses her hands*) My beloved . . . (HE *looks into her face*) For five years now I've been in love with you, and still I can't get used to it, and you seem more beautiful to me all the time. What marvelous, wonderful hair! What eyes! Tomorrow I'll take you away, we'll work, we'll be rich, my dreams will come true. You'll be happy. Only there's one thing wrong, just one thing wrong: you don't love me!

IRINA It isn't in my power! I'll be your wife, I'll be faithful and obedient, but it's not love, oh, what is there I can do? (SHE *cries*) I never have been in love in my life, not even once. Oh, I've dreamed so about love, dreamed about love so long now, day and night, but my soul is like some expensive piano that's locked and the key lost. (*A pause*) You look so worried.

TUZENBACH I didn't sleep all night. There isn't anything in my life terrible enough to frighten me, only that lost key tortures me, it won't let me sleep. Say something to me. (*A pause*) Say something to me. . . .

IRINA What? What is there to say? What?

TUZENBACH Something.

IRINA That's enough, that's enough! . . . (*A pause*)

TUZENBACH What senseless things, what idiotic little things suddenly, for no reason, start to matter in your life! You laugh at them the way you did before, you know they're senseless, and yet you go on and on and haven't the strength to stop. Oh, let's not talk about it! I'm happy. It's as if I were seeing for the first time in my life these firs and maples and birches, and they are all looking at me curiously and waiting. What beautiful trees, and how beautiful life ought to be under them! (*A shout:* "*Yoo-hoo!*") I must go, it's already time. . . . See that tree, it's dried up, but the wind moves it with the others just the same. So it seems to me that if I die, still, some way or other I'll have a share in life. Good-bye, my darling. . . . (HE *kisses her hands*) The papers you gave me are on my table under the calendar.

IRINA   I'm going with you.

TUZENBACH (*Uneasily*)   No, no! (HE *goes away quickly, then stops by the avenue of trees*) Irina!

IRINA   What?

TUZENBACH (*Not knowing what to say*)   I didn't have any coffee this morning. Tell them to make me some. . . .

[HE *goes out quickly.*

IRINA *stands lost in thought, then goes to the back of the stage and sits down in the swing.*

ANDREI *comes in with the baby carriage;* FERAPONT *appears.*]

FERAPONT   Andrei Sergeich, they're not my papers, you know, they're the government's. I didn't think them up.

ANDREI   Oh, where's it gone, what's become of it—my past, when I was young and gay and clever, when I had such beautiful dreams, such beautiful thoughts, when my present and future were bright with hope? Why is it that, almost before we've begun to live, we get boring, drab, uninteresting, lazy, indifferent, useless, unhappy? . . . Our town's been in existence for two hundred years, there's a hundred thousand people living in it, and there's not one of them that's not exactly the same as the others; there never has been in it, either in the past or in the present, a single saint, a single scholar, a single artist, a single person famous enough for anybody to envy him or try to be like him. . . . They just eat, drink, sleep, and then die. . . . And some more are born and they too eat, drink, sleep, and so as not to die of boredom they fill their lives with nasty gossip, vodka, cards, affairs, and the wives deceive their husbands and the husbands lie and pretend they don't see anything, and a kind of inexorable vulgarity oppresses the children, and the divine spark within them dies, and they become the same pitiful, absolutely identical corpses that their mothers and fathers were before them. . . . (*To* FERAPONT, *angrily*) What do you want?

FERAPONT  What? Papers to sign.

ANDREI  I'm sick of you.

FERAPONT  A while ago the doorman at the courthouse was saying—in Petersburg last winter, he says, it seems as how it was two hundred degrees below zero.

ANDREI  The present's disgusting, but on the other hand, when I think of the future—oh, then it's so good! I feel so light, so free: Off there in the distance the light dawns, I see freedom, I see my children and myself freed from laziness, from vodka, from goose with cabbage, from naps after dinner, from all this laziness and cowardice. . . .

FERAPONT  It seems as how two thousand people were frozen to death. He says people were terrified. Either it was Petersburg or Moscow, I don't remember.

ANDREI  (*Suddenly overcome with tenderness*) My own

darling sisters, my wonderful sisters . . . (*Tearfully*)
Masha, my own sister . . .

NATASHA   Who's that making all that noise out there?
Is that you, Andrei? You'll wake Baby Sophie! You know
you ought not to make any noise, Sophie's asleep. You're
as clumsy as a bear. If you want to talk, then give the
baby carriage and the baby to someone else! Ferapont,
take the baby carriage from your master.

FERAPONT   Yes'm.

ANDREI (*Embarrassed*)   I was speaking in a low voice.

NATASHA (*Behind the window, petting Bobik*)   Bobik!
Naughty Bobik! Bad Bobik!

ANDREI (*Glancing through the papers*)   All right, I'll
look them over and sign the ones that have to be signed,
and you can take them back to the board. . . .

[HE *goes into the house, reading the papers.*

FERAPONT *pushes the baby carriage toward the back
of the garden.*]

NATASHA   Bobik, tell Mother what's her name! You
darling, you darling! And who's that over there? That's
Aunt Olga. Say to your Aunt Olga: "How do you do,
Olga!"

[*Two street* MUSICIANS, *a* MAN *and a* GIRL, *come in
and begin to play on a violin and harp;* VERSHININ, OLGA,
*and* ANFISA *come out of the house and listen silently
for a moment;* IRINA *comes up*]

OLGA   Our garden's like a vacant lot, they walk right
through it. Nurse dear, give the musicians something.

ANFISA (*Giving something to the* MUSICIANS)   Good-bye

and God bless you! (*The* Musicians *bow and go out*)
Poor things! If you've enough to eat you don't go around
playing. (*To* Irina) Good morning, little Irina! (She
*kisses her*) M-m-m-m, child, the life I lead! the life I lead!
At the high school in a lovely government apartment,
there with little Olga—that's what the Lord has vouchsafed
me in my old age! Sinner that I am, never in my whole
life have I lived the way I live now! . . . A big apartment,
a government one, and I've a little room all to myself,
a little bed—all government property! I go to sleep at
night and—O Lord! Mother of God, there's nobody in
the whole world happier than I am!

Vershinin   We're leaving right away, Olga Sergeevna.
It's time I was going. (*A pause*) I wish you everything,
everything. . . . Where is Marya Sergeevna?

Irina   She's somewhere in the garden. I'll go look for her.

Vershinin   Please do. I haven't much time.

Anfisa   I'll go look too. (She *calls*) Little Masha, yoo-
hoo! (She *goes with* Irina *toward the back of the garden*)
Yoo-hoo! Yoo-hoo!

Vershinin   Everything comes to an end. And so we too
must part. (He *looks at his watch*) The town gave us
a sort of lunch, we drank champagne, the mayor made a
speech, I ate and listened, but my soul was here with
you. . . . (He *looks around the garden*) I'll miss you.

Olga   Shall we see each other again, someday?

Vershinin   Most likely not. (*A pause*) My wife and my
two little girls will be staying for two months more;
please, if anything should happen, if they should need
anything . . .

Olga   Yes, yes, of course. Don't even think about it.

(*A pause*) By tomorrow there won't be a single soldier left in town, it will all be only a memory—and of course a new life will begin for us. . . . (*A pause*) Nothing turns out the way we want it to. I didn't want to be a headmistress, and just the same I've become one. It means we won't live in Moscow. . . .

VERSHININ  Well. . . . Thank you for everything. Forgive me if anything wasn't what it should have been. . . . I've talked a lot, such a lot—and forgive me for that, don't hold it against me. . . .

OLGA (*Wiping her eyes*)  Why doesn't Masha come on . . .

VERSHININ  What is there left for me to say to you, in farewell? What's left to philosophize about? . . . (HE *laughs*) Life is hard. It seems to many of us lonely and hopeless—but just the same you've got to admit it's gradually getting clearer and lighter, and plainly the time isn't too far away when it will be entirely bright. (HE *looks at his watch*) It's time for me to leave, it's time! In the old days mankind was busy with wars, its whole existence was filled with campaigns, invasions, conquests, but nowadays we've outlived all that. It's left behind an enormous vacuum which, so far, there is nothing to fill; mankind is passionately searching for it and of course will find it. Ah, if only it would come more quickly! (*A pause*) You know, if only industry could be added to education, and education to industry . . . (HE *looks at his watch*) But it's time I was going. . . .

OLGA  Here she comes.

VERSHININ  I came to say good-bye. . . .

[OLGA *goes off a little to the side, in order to let them say good-bye*]

MASHA (*Looking into his face*)   Good-bye. . . . (A long kiss)

OLGA   There, there . . . (MASHA *is sobbing violently*)

VERSHININ   Write me. . . . Don't forget me! Let me go . . . it's time. . . . Olga Sergeevna, take her, I'm already . . . it's time . . . I'm late . . .

[*Moved,* HE *kisses* OLGA's *hands, then once again embraces* MASHA *and quickly goes out*]

OLGA   There, Masha, there. . . . Stop, darling. . . .

[KULYGIN *enters*]

KULYGIN (*Embarrassed*)   It's all right, let her cry, let her. . . . My good Masha, my sweet Masha. . . . You're my wife, and I'm happy, no matter what happens. . . . I don't complain, I don't reproach you for a single thing. There's Olga, she'll be our witness. . . . Let's start over and live the way we used to, and I won't by so much as a single word, by the least hint . . .

MASHA (*Stifling her sobs*)   By the curved seastrand a green oak stands, /
A chain of gold upon it . . . a chain of gold upon it . . . I'm going out of my mind. . . . By the curved seastrand . . . a green oak . . .

OLGA   Hush, Masha. . . . Hush. . . . Give her some water.

MASHA   I'm not crying any more. . . .

KULYGIN   She's not crying any more. . . . She's a good girl. . . .

[*A muffled, far-off shot is heard*]

MASHA   By the curved seastrand a green oak stands, /
A chain of gold upon it . . . a green cat . . . a green oak
. . . I'm all mixed up. . . . (SHE *takes a drink of water*)
My life's all wrong. I don't want anything any more. . . .
I'll be all right in a minute. . . . What difference is
anything anyway? . . . What does it mean, *by the curved
seastrand?* Why do I keep saying that? My thoughts
are all mixed up.

[IRINA *enters*]

OLGA   Hush, Masha. Now you're being a sensible girl.
. . . Let's go on in. . . .
MASHA (*Angrily*)   I won't go in there. (SHE *sobs, but
immediately stops herself*) I don't go in that house any
more, and I won't now. . . .
IRINA   Let's just sit together for a while and not say
anything. . . . Tomorrow I'm going, you know. . . .
KULYGIN   Yesterday I took this moustache and beard
away from one of the boys in my class. . . . (HE *puts on
the moustache and beard*) I look just like the German
teacher. . . . (HE *laughs*) Don't I? They're funny, those
boys. . . .
MASHA   You really do look just like that German of yours.
OLGA (*Laughing*)   You do. (MASHA *cries*)
IRINA   There, Masha, there!
KULYGIN   Just like . . .

[NATASHA *comes in*]

NATASHA (*To the maid*)   What? Protopopov's going to
sit with Baby Sophie, and Andrei Sergeevich can take

Bobik for a ride. Children are so much trouble. . . . (*To* IRINA) Irina, you're leaving tomorrow—such a pity! Do stay at least one week more! (SHE *catches sight of* KULYGIN *and shrieks;* HE *laughs and takes off his moustache and beard*)What on earth—get out, how you did scare me! (*To Irina*) I'll miss you—do you think having you leave is going to be easy for me? I've told them to put Andrei and his violin in your room—let him saw away in there!—and we're going to put Baby Sophie in his room. That wonderful, marvelous child! What a girl! Today she looked up at me with the most extraordinary expression in her eyes and—"Mama!"

KULYGIN   A beautiful child, that's so.

NATASHA   So tomorrow I'll be all alone here. (SHE *sighs*) First of all I'm going to have them chop down all those fir trees along the walk, and then that maple. . . . In the evening it's so ugly. . . . (*To* IRINA) Dear, that belt isn't a bit becoming to you. . . . It's in bad taste—you need something a little brighter. . . . And I'm having them plant darling little flowers everywhere—how they will smell! (*Sternly*) What's this fork doing lying around on this bench? (SHE *goes into the house; to the* MAID) Will you tell me what this fork is doing lying around on this bench? (SHE *shouts*) Don't you dare talk back to me!

KULYGIN   There she goes again!

[*Behind the scene a band is playing a march;* EVERYBODY *listens*]

OLGA   They are leaving.

[SHE *goes away.*

CHEBUTYKIN *comes in.*]

MASHA   Our friends are leaving. Well, let's wish them a happy journey! (*To her* HUSBAND) We must go home. Where are my hat and cape?

KULYGIN   I took them indoors. . . . I'll get them right away.

[HE *goes into the house*]

OLGA   Yes, now we can all go home. It's time.

CHEBUTYKIN   Olga Sergeevna!

OLGA   What is it? (*A pause*) What is it?

CHEBUTYKIN   Nothing. . . . I don't know how to tell you. . . . (HE *whispers in her ear*)

OLGA (*Alarmed*)   It's not possible!

CHEBUTYKIN   Yes. . . . What a mess! . . . I'm worn out, I'm sick and tired of it. I don't want to say another word. . . . (*Irritably*) Anyway, what's the difference!

MASHA   What's happened?

OLGA (*Putting her arms around* IRINA)   This is a terrible day. I don't know how to tell you, my darling. . . .

IRINA   What? Tell me right away, what? For God's sake! (SHE *cries*)

CHEBUTYKIN   A little while ago the Baron was killed in a duel.

IRINA (*Crying softly*)   I knew, I knew. . . .

CHEBUTYKIN (*Sitting down on a bench at the back of the stage*) I'm worn out. . . . (HE *takes a newspaper out of his pocket*) Let 'em cry. . . . (HE *sings softly*) Ta-ra-ra-boom-de-aye . . . / Sit on a log I may . . . What's the difference anyway? (*The* THREE SISTERS *stand nestled against one another*)

MASHA   Oh, how the music is playing! They are leaving us, one is really gone, really, gone forever and ever; we'll stay here alone, to begin our life over again. We must live . . . we must live . . .

IRINA (*Putting her head on* OLGA's *breast*)   The time will come when everyone will know why all this is, what these sufferings are for, there will be no more secrets— but in the meantime we must live . . . must work, only work! Tomorrow I'll go away alone, I'll teach in the school and give my life to those who'll need it, perhaps. It's fall now, soon the winter will come and cover everything with snow, and I will work, I will work . . .

OLGA (*Putting her arms around both her* SISTERS)   The music is playing so gaily, so eagerly, and one wants so to live! Oh, my God! Time will pass, and we shall be gone forever, they will forget us—they'll forget our faces, our voices, and how many of us there were, but our sufferings will change into joy for those who will live after us, happiness and peace will come on earth, and they'll be reminded and speak tenderly of those who are living now, they will bless them. Oh, dear sisters, our life isn't over yet. We shall live! The music is playing so gaily, so joyfully, and it seems as though a little more and we shall know why we live, why we suffer. . . . If only we knew, if only we knew!

[*The music grows fainter and fainter;* KULYGIN, *smiling happily, brings the hat and cape;* ANDREI *pushes* BOBIK *across the stage in the baby carriage*]

*Masha, Irina, and Olga*
*Photograph by* MARTHA HOLMES

CHEBUTYKIN (*Singing softly*)    Ta-ra-ra-boom-de-aye.
Sit on a log I may . . . (HE *reads the newspaper*) What's
the difference anyway! What's the difference!
OLGA   If only we knew, if only we knew!

CURTAIN

# AFTERWORD

ABOUT TRANSLATING OF ANY KIND RANDALL JARRELL liked
to quote Chekhov's "When I read other people's trans-
lations I am always changing and shifting the words
around mentally and I get something light and ethereal
like lace." In 1953 he chose *The Three Sisters* not only
because it was his favorite Chekhov play; it was his favorite
play. He'd been thinking about it as a play long before
he made up his mind to translate it, and he never really
stopped thinking about it.

He wrote about many writers and cared about many
more, but the one he thought of as being the closest to his
own nature as an artist and a man was Chekhov. At the
time of Randall Jarrell's death in 1965 there were nearly
one hundred handwritten pages of notes for an essay on
*The Three Sisters* that he meant to write for this book.
On these pages he wrote what he got from reading
Chekhov and about Chekhov over the years: that is, his own
feeling for Chekhov's intentions, and his own way of
looking at this play. The notes were *notes*: rough and
preliminary, but crammed with opinions. Randall would
have edited these and rewritten them, and reedited and
rewritten until he made a finished prose piece about
*The Three Sisters*. Myself, I could do none of this—least
of all discard one word. I did try with some "changing
and shifting" to get an order of form that would make
them usable to actors especially, and any others who want

to think about the play in detail. Also, for the sake of coherence I contributed some lines here and there in as nearly Randall Jarrell's words as I could.

Working daily for some months with his handwriting and his thoughts has been a fond assignment for me and—though I longed to finish—I am sorry to come to the end of it.

MARY JARRELL

*May 6, 1968*

*About* THE THREE SISTERS:

# NOTES

# I / CHEKHOV AND THE PLAY

IN A SENSE *The Three Sisters* needs criticism less than almost any play I can think of. It is so marvelously organized, made, realized, that reading it or seeing it many times to be thoroughly acquainted with it is all one needs. In it Chekhov gives us a cluster of attitudes about values—happiness, marriage, work, duty, beauty, cultivation, the past, the present, the future—and shows us how these are meaningful or meaningless to people. Values are presented to us through opposed opinions, opposed lives; at different ages in life with different emotions; and finally, on different levels.

Take the ways, for instance, that marriage is presented: so obviously, so tenuously, so alternatively. All the marriages we see are disasters; but Vershinin's goes wrong for different reasons than Andrei's, and Andrei's goes wrong for different reasons than Masha's. Still, Chekhov can lump them into one generalization that we accept when Vershinin says, "Why is a Russian always sick and tired of his wife . . . and his wife and children always sick and tired of him?" Then he uses a generalization from particular experience when he has Andrei tell us, "People shouldn't get married. They shouldn't because it's boring." These are bold truths. And yet, surrounded by bad models (and in Kulygin's case, involved in one), Olga remains convincingly dedicated to marriage as an ideal—woman's role, woman's duty. And Kulygin never loses his faith in its value as a value, or as an "institution" to belong to for its own sake, and continues to encourage the single ones to marry.

"Love and Marriage" is a little ballet for Irina and Tuzenbach of coming together and parting, of going separate ways yet looking over shoulders. First they are on the same side about love. Both of them idealize it and want it, but while his dream of love is Irina, hers is Moscow where she'll meet "the real one." Later, when

she gives up her dream, they come together on the marriage
level (long enough to be engaged) but not at the love level. Theirs
is a poignant pas de deux when, first, Irina truthfully declares
it is not in her power to love this homely man and, after that,
Tuzenbach's own sensitive drawing back from marriage on those
terms. Both of them achieve their maximum substance as human
beings at this moment. When he says to her, "There isn't anything
in my life terrible enough to frighten me, only that lost key . . ."
(the key to Irina's love), and when he puts love ahead of the
imminent duel, Tuzenbach is ennobled. The ambiguities here make
it possible for us to wonder whether the marriage would really
have gone ahead the next day if he had not been killed, whether
the "dead tree" allusion of Tuzenbach's meant he *knew* (by
willing it) that he was going to die.

Chekhov was nearly forty when he fell deeply in love with the
actress Olga Knipper. He wrote Masha's part for her, and,
significantly, love and marriage are examined in this play more
than any other. The fact he had not married all this while is an
indication of sorts, but of course, the stories tell us over and over
in fiction what he often told his friends in letters. At age twenty-
five he wrote, "I am above marriage." Ten years later he wrote,
"Very well, I'll marry if you wish it. But here are my conditions:
Everything must remain the same as before—that is she must live
in Moscow and I in the country, and I'll make visits to her. The
kind of happiness which continues day in and day out, from one
morning to the next, I cannot endure. When people tell me the
same thing in the same tone of voice every day, I become
furious. . . . I promise to be a splendid husband, but give me a
wife who, like the moon, will not appear in my sky every day."
In a letter to his brother Misha, advising him on Misha's marriage,
Chekhov wrote that the absolute essential was "love, sexual
attraction, to be one flesh."

When the play was finished he and Olga Knipper were married,
but in the months beforehand he delayed it by every possible
tactic until she made it plain he could not hold her without it.
Shortly after, he wrote his sister (five years later than the other
letter about his "conditions" for marriage) and said, "That I'm

married, you already know. I don't think the fact will in any way
change my life or the conditions under which I have lived up to
now . . . everything will go on as before. At the end of July
I'll be in Yalta, then in Moscow until December, and then back
in Yalta. That is, my wife and I will live apart—a situation, by the
way, to which I'm already accustomed." Partly accustomed, yes;
and the marriage went ahead along the lines he'd laid down earlier,
but not as easily as he'd assumed. He did get much writing done
by himself in Yalta where he had to stay at times in the milder
climate on account of his tuberculosis, but also he got bored and
lonely. Among many letters to Olga (they wrote every day) he
once said, "I keep waiting for you to order me to pack and travel
to Moscow. To Moscow! To Moscow! that is not said by *three
sisters* but by one husband." In *The Three Sisters* many voices
tell us what he'd summarized in one sentence in 1898 in the
story *About Love*: "The one incontestable truth about love is
that it is a mystery and all that is written about it is not a solution
but a series of questions that remain unanswered."

THERE IS A REAL GEOMETRY TO *The Three Sisters*. It has an
ideological, character, and chain-of-events organization that
develops with an inevitableness akin to Greek tragedy. After making
his logical skeleton Chekhov invents and *invents* plausible disguises
that keep the play from having the Ibsen-well-made surface and
the symbols from having the Ibsen starkness. Indeed, having so
many symbols and leitmotivs prevents the most important of any
of them from sticking out or being too differentiated from the
rest of the surface. While the underlying organization is extremely
plain, parallel, and symmetrical, it is masked by a "spot-surface"
or expressed in terms of these "spots" themselves.

A visual counterpart of this very method uncannily exists in the
work of the painter Vuillard. In certain of his indoor and outdoor
scenes of French domestic life, the foundation areas on the canvas
are made less emphatic by the swarms of particles that mottle the
walls with rose-printed paper, the rugs with swirls, the lawns
with pools of sun and shade. From such variation and variegation
comes his cohesion. Vuillard commingles plaids and dappled things

as non sequitur as the jottings in Chebutykin's notebook. He
alludes to a mysterious darkness by leaving a door ajar. He baffles
the viewer by a woman's ear glowing red. What does she hear?
In the same way, Masha's eccentric line "By the curved seastrand
a green oak stands/   A chain of gold upon it . . ." baffles us.
What *does* it mean?

These Vuillard "spots" are found in bizarre, grotesque, homey
touches in a speech, a mannerism, a trait, an incident that add up to
several dozen possibly. Solyony, Chebutykin, Kulygin, Natasha,
and Ferapont are covered with them; Olga and Irina and Vershinin
scarcely have any; with Masha and Tuzenbach they are used
sparingly but memorably. Chekhov made such imaginative and
original use of the indeterminacy principle on the microscopic
level (the opposite of Ibsen) while maintaining on the macroscopic
level firm causality. The more his themes and characters were
contradictory, inconsistent, and ambiguous, the more the play got
a feeling of the randomness and personalness of real life.


## VUILLARD SPOTS

### *Act* 1

SOLYONY. With one hand I can only lift sixty pounds, but with
    both hands I can lift a hundred and eighty—two hundred, even.
    From that I deduce that two men aren't twice as strong, they're
    three times as strong as one man, etc.
CHEBUTYKIN: For falling hair: Two ounces of naphtha in half a
    pint of alcohol, etc.
SOLYONY: . . . you'll die of apoplexy or I'll lose control of myself
    and put a bullet through your head, my angel.
MASHA: By the curved seastrand a green oak stands, etc.
SOLYONY: Before he'd time to get his breath/ The bear was hugging
    him to death, etc.
FERAPONT: How's that? (*Deafness.*)
ANFISA: Irina, darling, now you be a nice polite little girl.

MASHA: The love-sick major, etc.

SOLYONY: Because if the station were here, it wouldn't be way off there, etc.

SOLYONY: Here chick-chicky (*repeated*).

CHEBUTYKIN: Male and female created He them!

KULYGIN: (*Repeating the gift of the book and using Latin tags.*)

KULYGIN: The rugs must be taken up for the summer, the moth balls, *mens sana in corpore sano*, etc.

CHEBUTYKIN: With newspapers and combing his beard.

KULYGIN: C-minus in deportment, etc.

SOLYONY: Cockroaches.

FEDOTIK: Photographs, gift, top.

MASHA: (*Again*) By the curved seastrand, etc.

### Act II

FERAPONT: The forty pancakes.

The rope over Moscow.

MASHA: The wind in the chimney.

CHEBUTYKIN: (Knocking on the floor.)

For eight months, not a kopeck, evidently he's forgotten.

MASHA: Ever since morning I've been laughing.

CHEBUTYKIN: Balzac was married in Berdichev.

FEDOTIK: Giving the crayons and penknife to Irina.

Showing her a new kind of solitaire.

Telling her she isn't "going out" in the game so she won't get to Moscow.

CHEBUTYKIN: Tsitsikar—smallpox is raging there.

SOLYONY: Fry that baby in the frying pan.

TUZENBACH: What's become of the candy? Solyony ate it.

VERSHININ: My wife's poisoned herself again.

MASHA: Mixing up Irina's cards and spoiling her game.

SOLYONY: Ah, be not wroth, Aleko.

CHEBUTYKIN: Chekhartma-cheremsha.

TUZENBACH-ANDREI-CHEBUTYKIN: "My New Porch" song.

Solyony's perfume.

SOLYONY-ANDREI: Argument about two universities in Moscow.

MASHA: The Baron's drunk (*waltzing to herself*).
Troika with bells, carnival people's voices.
KULYGIN: *O, fallacem hominum spem!* Accusative of exclamation.
Accordion in street, nurse singing.

## Act III

Sound effects with fire: gathering of clothes, ringing, etc.
FERAPONT: Moscow, the French were flabbergasted.
MASHA: (*Goes out angrily with her pillow*).
KULYGIN: (*Hides behind a wardrobe*).
CHEBUTYKIN: Smashes clock.
KULYGIN: Zero-minus in deportment.
SOLYONY: More perfume-sprinkling: "T'would annoy the geese, I fear."
    More chicky-chicky, etc.
KULYGIN: I'm satisfied. I'm satisfied. I'm satisfied.
MASHA: Bored, bored, bored!
ANFISA: Don't throw me out.
IRINA: I can't remember what window is in Italian.
OLGA: He (*Tuzenbach*) looked so homely I wanted to cry. (*She cries.*)
MASHA: (*About Natasha*) She walks like the one who started the fire.
OLGA: (*About Masha*) The silliest one in the family, that's you.
OLGA: (*When Masha is confessing her love affair*) Anyway I don't hear you. I don't hear what silly things you are saying.
MASHA: Like Gogol's madman—silence—silence.
CHEBUTYKIN: Knocking on the floor again.

## Act IV

FEDOTIK: Oh, stand still!
RODE: Good-bye echo. Good-bye trees.
KULYGIN: Your Polish wife will call you *kochany*.
CHEBUTYKIN: He puts a newspaper in a pocket and takes a newspaper out of a pocket.

Gu-Gu-God-fearing man.

Ta-ra-ra-boom-de-aye . . . / Sit on a log I may, etc.

KULYGIN: With a moustache, or without a moustache, I'm satisfied.

KULYGIN: Nonsense. Nonesuch.

All the yoo-hoos in the act.

KULYGIN: *Ut consecutivum* anecdote.

"The Maiden's Prayer" at the piano.

MASHA TO CHEBUTYKIN: And she loved you? (He): I don't know.

MASHA: Is my man here?

Chebutykin's old-fashioned watch that strikes.

CHEBUTYKIN: Piff-paff.

Noticing the swans and geese flying south.

SOLYONY: Before he'd time to get his breath/ The bear was hugging, etc.

Perfume sprinkling on his hands.

Tuzenbach's straw hat. Tell them to make some coffee, as last words.

FERAPONT: Petersburg or Moscow it was. Two hundred degrees below zero.

Two thousand people froze to death.

ANFISA: A little room, a little bed—all government property, etc.

AN ESSENTIAL PART OF THE PLAY is the meaning of life as opposed to the meaninglessness of life. Chekhov shows us what people say, believe, believe under their acts (unconsciously) until *The Three Sisters* becomes a poll of answers about his values and ultimates. How *many* answers there are and how paradoxical Chekhov thought they were can be seen immediately if they are listed as follows:

## THEMES

| MEANING | MEANINGLESSNESS |
|---|---|
| *Specific meaning:* Knowledge, the meaningful past, Moscow, father. | "What's the difference?" nonsense, stupidity, silliness, crudeness, provincial present. |
| Remembering this. | Forgetting, denying, departing. |
| Happiness: through love, dreams, work, progress, ("If only"-dreams). | Unhappiness: frustration, boredom, "work without poetry," loneliness, empty dutifulness. |
| Satisfactions: work, progress, duty. | Despair at lack of progress or slowness of it. |
| Fate or lot: accepting this, "We must live," "We shall live." | The life we reconcile ourselves to, nihilism, "What's the difference?" "It's all the same." |
| Dreams-wishes: dreams are necessary. | Tiredness, exhaustion, headaches due to weariness in waiting for dreams to come true, giving up on dreams. |
| Love. | Lack of love. |
| Youth. | Age and aging. |

IN A CERTAIN SENSE *The Three Sisters* is as well-made as an Ibsen play in that everything is related to everything else, except that Chekhov relates things in a musical way, or in a realistic-causal, rather than geometrical-rhetorical-causal, way. The repeated use of Wagnerian leitmotivs occurs not only for characters but for themes, ideology, and morality. Diffusing the themes required more concentration, he wrote in letters when he was working on *The Three Sisters*, than for any other play. He perfected it to relax the essential structural framework the play is built on. In the exchange of themes, overly defined edges of characterization and situation are blurred and, to him, more realistic. In particular,

Chebutykin's "What's the difference?" is his own special leitmotiv that, however, is borrowed by nearly everyone at sometime or other, just as themes of fatigue, happiness, boredom, etc., are shared.

Loneliness (hardly a value or a philosophy) becomes a sort of ghost that haunts Andrei all the time, Irina until she gets older, and Solyony under cover of his Lermontov personality. Loneliness pervaded Chekhov's own life in similar ways. He wrote someone, "I positively cannot live without guests. When I am alone, for some reason I become terrified, just as though I were in a frail little boat on a great ocean." Though he kept people around him a lot of the time, there was an essential distance from, removal of everybody else from Chekhov in life. He joked and played jokes and behaved frivolously as a regular way of getting along with people. Even when he was so in love with Olga Knipper, it was hard for him to stay close, and he'd write her "silly" letters that she sometimes scolded him for. She wanted him to talk of the meaning of life once, and he wrote her (à la Tuzenbach's "See it's snowing" sentence), "You ask: What is life? That is just the same as asking: What is a carrot? A carrot is a carrot, and nothing more is known about it." For years he wore a seal ring with these words: "To the lonely man the world is a desert."

He keeps us conscious of the loneliness underneath the general animation. At the birthday party in Act I, there is Vershinin's line about the gloomy-looking bridge in Moscow where the water under it could be heard: "It makes a lonely man feel sad." Later on we hear again when Chebutykin tells Andrei about being unmarried, even if marriage is boring: "But the loneliness! You can philosophize as much as you please, but loneliness is a terrible thing, Andrei. . . ." With the "good-bye trees" and "good-bye echo" and the embraces, tears, *au revoir*'s and farewells, loneliness has built up like entropy as the good social group—that partly kept people from being lonely—has been broken into by the inferior outside world. The organized enclave of Act I, after being invaded by the relatively unorganized environment, loses its own organization like a physical system and runs down to almost nothing . . . Andrei.

The musical side of Russian life, and Chekhov, comes into the
play in every act: Masha whistles, the carnival people play offstage, Chebutykin sings nervously after the duel. Specifically,
Act I opens with Olga remembering the band's funeral march
after the father's death and Act IV ends with the band playing a
march as the brigade leaves and Olga has her last, summarizing
speech. The "yoo-hoos" beforehand have imparted a faintly musical
nostalgia to the scene, too. In Acts I and II there are guitar and
piano and singing. "My New Porch" is a song everyone knows
like "Old MacDonald Had a Farm," so that when Tuzenbach
starts it off, even lonely Andrei and old Chebutykin can carry it
along. Masha and Vershinin's duet becomes a witty—but entirely
different—parallel of this formula. The camaraderie at the bottom
of the first is countered with the romantic insinuation of the
second. "Unto love all ages bow, its pangs are blest . . ." leaves
nothing in doubt, and when Masha sings a refrain of this and
Vershinin adds another, they make a musical declaration of love.
This is an excellent preparation for Act III when, after Masha's
love confession, it would have been awkward for Vershinin and
her to appear together on stage. Their intimacy is even strength-
ened, in our minds, by his off-stage song to Masha which she hears,
comprehends, and answers in song before leaving the stage to join
him.

There was always a piano in Chekhov's house, and having someone play helped him to write when he got stuck. Rhythms came
naturally to him, and just as he has varied them in the lines of
*The Three Sisters*—from the shortest (sounds, single words) to
the arias and big set speeches—similarly there is a rhythmic pattern
like that on a railway platform where all the people know each
other and little groups leave, say good-bye, meet.

To ME, Davchenko's comment on the lack of spontaneity of this
play is really a tribute to its extraordinary solidity of construction.
How frail, spontaneously lyric, and farcical *The Cherry Orchard*
is in comparison. Chekhov said of it, "I call it a comedy." It was
the work of a dying man who had strength to write only a few

lines a day, whereas *The Three Sisters: A Drama in Four Acts*
is his crowning work. It is the culmination of his whole writing
life. *Uncle Vanya* is the nearest thing, but nothing equally long
(none of the short novels) is as good as *The Three Sisters*.

# II / THE SETTING

WHAT PEOPLE REMEMBER FROM *The Three Sisters*, if they have
forgotten everything else, is Irina's "To Moscow! To Moscow!
To Moscow!" But few of us know, as audiences at the Moscow
Art Theatre in 1900 knew, the all-or-nothing cultural contrast
between living in Moscow or living in a provincial Russian city.
As for Moscow we can rely somewhat on our imaginations, but
for the Protopopov world that is the setting for *The Three Sisters*,
our imagination comes off nowhere and only Chekhov's own
words can give us the knowledge of it that we need. Here is
Chekhov's description of a provincial city of a hundred thousand
people, or more, like the one where the Prozorov household lived:

> I DID NOT KNOW ONE HONEST PERSON in the entire town. My father
> took bribes and thought they were being given him out of
> respect for his spiritual qualities. In order to be promoted from
> one class to another, students went to board with their teachers,
> who grossly overcharged them for it. The wife of the military
> commander accepted money from the recruits at enlistment
> time and even allowed them to entertain her, she was once so
> drunk in church that she was totally unable to get up from her
> knees. Doctors accepted money too, at recruitment time, and
> the town doctor and the veterinarian levied a tax on butcher
> shops and inn. At the district college there was a brisk trade
> in certificates granting military exemptions for the third school
> year. The higher clergy accepted money from their subordinates
> and the church elders. At the town council, the citizens'
> council, the medical board and all similar boards, the cry, "You
> have to give thanks!" followed every petitioner, and the
> petitioner would return to give thirty or forty kopecks. And
> those who did not take bribes, dignitaries of the Department of
> Justice, for example, were haughty, extended two fingers for a
> handshake; distinguished themselves by their coldness and

narrowness of judgment, played cards a great deal, drank copiously, married rich women, and undoubtedly had a harmful, corrupting influence on society. Only from some of the younger girls was there a breath of moral purity. The majority of them had lofty aspirations and honest, pure souls, but they had no knowledge of life and believed bribes were given out of respect for spiritual qualities; on marrying, they aged rapidly, let themselves go, and sank hopelessly into the mire of a vulgar, plebeian existence.

In the shops, the tradesmen used to unload their rotten meat, musty flour, and left-over tea on us workers; in the churches, the police shoved us around, in the hospitals, the doctors' assistants and nurses fleeced us, and if we were too poor to bribe them, they would feed us from dirty dishes in revenge; in the postoffice the pettiest clerk felt he had the right to treat us like animals. . . . But what struck me most of all in my new position was the total absence of justice, the very thing popularly expressed by the words: "They've forgotten God." A day rarely went by without swindling. . . . We always had to ask for the money we earned as if it were charity—standing cap in hand by the back stairs.

*from* MY LIFE, *1896*

# III / THE CHARACTERS

| | |
|---|---|
| OLGA | TUZENBACH |
| IRINA | SOLYONY |
| MASHA | NATASHA |
| ANDREI | FEDOTIK |
| CHEBUTYKIN | RODE |
| VERSHININ | FERAPONT |
| KULYGIN | ANFISA |

## OLGA

*And this life was making her grow old and coarse, making her ugly, angular, and awkward . . .*
                                    *from* THE SCHOOLMISTRESS, *1897*

PROPERTIES: The past, papers to correct, uniform, dream of Moscow, dream of marriage, headaches, exhaustion, headmistress post, government apartment, Anfisa.

HOW SHE MAKES LIFE MEANINGFUL: By living up to the code of *noblesse oblige*, i.e., noble rank requires noble conduct. By teaching from a sense of duty, not desire. By carrying on the household after the father's death, just as she'd stepped into the mother's place after the mother's death. By dreaming of Moscow —not so much the physical city, as Andrei did, but more Moscow as their past—where, if they could just get back to it, she feels sure a young woman of her age and of good family would not be teaching school and having the strength and youth "squeezed out day by day, drop by drop," but be married and stay home all day.

OLGA IS THE MORALLY SUPERIOR WOMAN IN THE PLAY, just as
Tuzenbach is the morally superior man. Her long introductory
speeches are those of the custodian of the family memories. And
she, more than the others, believes in the rehabilitation of their past
in Moscow. Partly she is having to take the place of the father
now, but she is not an authority or power figure; she is simply the
oldest sister acting in a gently supervisory manner. When she
flies out at Masha, we know this is due to the irritability and
headaches caused by her work; still she has the right amount of
correcting-older-sister tone. She has an essentially warm, caring-
for-others, womanly nature—not as self-interested as Masha and
Irina—and wants to see good in life, tries to take what comes as
God's will, and is still hopeful that it is God's will they go to
Moscow. When her headache passes, we see her at her best, being
hospitable, announcing lunch, mothering Irina, and assuming
domestic responsibility.

In Act I she is the hostess. She wants things to go smoothly in
their (the Prozorovs') home. Her incident with Natasha and the
belt shows Olga wants to befriend Natasha and spare her from
the critical comments of Masha and others. She is not trying to
be interfering and would happily give Natasha her own belt if
she had one. The "wrong" belt was just one of the aesthetic
clichés, almost with the force of morality—like a woman covering
her head in church—that any woman would help another with.

In Act II Olga's psychosomatic weariness and headaches are
acute and drive her off the scene and straight to bed.

In Act III we see her disinterestedness established. At the time
of Natasha's first speech on entering Olga and Irina's room, the
stage directions for Olga are: (*Not listening to her*). When Masha
begins her declaration of love for Vershinin, all of Olga's lines
have to do with not listening and she even retires from sight
behind a screen. When Andrei wants to talk out "what it is you've
got against me," Olga very decidedly says, "Let it go now, Andrei
dear. We'll settle things tomorrow." This genteel procrastination
is used by Masha in Act I when she is depressed and wants to
go home and says they'll talk about it "afterwards." Irina, too,
has a version of it in Act IV when Masha is upset and crying over

Vershinin's departure and Irina says, "Let's just sit together for
a while and not say anything. . . ." In its dispersal among the
sisters, it seems as if this tendency were a euphemism of manners,
taught by Mother and the environment to postpone troubling
matters as long as possible (on the chance of avoiding them
entirely).

In Olga's case this trait is a furthering of the gentility we already
know her for and coincides with the shock she experiences from
Natasha's rudeness to Anfisa. In the Natasha-Olga quarrel Chekhov
is opposing ruthlessness with gentility. It is not the rebellious and
spirited Masha nor the mercurial and emotional Irina whom he
selects to do this—for they might not be able to control themselves
enough to keep their voices down and make the ladylike protests
Olga makes. When Olga says that the *least* rudeness, even an
impolite word, upsets her and that she doesn't have the strength
to bear it . . . and that everything is getting black before her eyes
and she is ready to faint, it would be ludicrous to have these lines
shouted. Olga would no more raise her voice in this discussion
than Natasha would lower hers. This becomes an excellent means
of clarifying in a very specific way our knowledge of the gulf
between the Prozorov world and the Protopopov world.

Olga's headaches are gone in Act III and also her dreams of
Moscow. She is still tired and drained by her circumstances and by
her high ethics in giving to others (not only charity for the fire
victims but counsel and comfort to her family)—giving, giving,
and receiving so little. Surrounded as she is by persons with
"lower aims" (adultery, drunkenness, gambling, unkindness, even
adolescent emotionalism) than hers, it is hard for Olga, for a while,
to see only good in life and accept all this as God's will. In her
benevolent counsel to Irina to marry the Baron, Olga thinks of
marriage for herself once more and says aloud her little, last,
childlike prayer that love would not be necessary, God dear, just
any decent man who proposed, ". . . an old man, even. . . ."
Marriage, any kind at all, that would take her away is crucial to
Olga since the quarrel with Natasha. This was her particular
climax when, after such rudeness and the vision of more, Olga sees
that the Prozorov enclave of cultivation is simply a barbarian

household (with Andrei its one helpless, cultivated slave) and that she has to leave it entirely.

A delicate manifestation of Chekhovian, drawn-from-life writing in the play is the appealing bond between the in-laws Olga and Kulygin. Not only is their mutual exhaustion from their similar endeavors at the school Kulygin's biggest conversational point with her, but their shared loyalty to marriage is of even more significance. All the marriages we see are disastrous. Still, these two continue to think it desirable and both of them have many remarks about marrying. Rooted in the past as Olga is, she holds fast (against the beginning fad to the contrary) to the idea that woman's place is in the home. Unlike Irina who *wants* to work and Masha who is so marriage-weary, Olga thinks marriage gives a woman status, is what she was placed on earth for, and that to be husbandless is to be homeless, which, indeed, in the end is Olga's fate. Kulygin's attitudes are different, but it is rather striking that, in the midst of his own precariously difficult marriage, he can still think of that institution as a source for happiness and come out with such a sentence as, "I often think if it hadn't been Masha I'd have married you, Olga dear. You have such a generous nature. . . ."

In Act IV Olga has escaped from even her "tired" remarks. And this helps to make her seem better off and accustomed to her life. With no more lines about marriage, or "I suffer, too," we feel she has become reconciled to life on this level. She has changed out of her psychosomatic misery and her wanting to give away everything to an essentially calm and disinterested person resigned to an impersonal life. All this prepares us for her final speech. Throughout the play she has served her *noblesse oblige* and it has served her. As someone has said, "What we give ourselves to, we become." So now she is the appropriate one to speak last and sum up the play. Whereas in the beginning her present was made endurable by her dreams of the past, in the end her speeches are all linked to the future, a future not of secular progress like Vershinin's, but a religious future. When she puts her arms around her sisters to say some sentences of consolation, Olga has her big aria about remembrance. Partly she is saying they *will* pass and be forgotten, but also, that in the end, remembrance exists, and not forgetting. She tells them that some meaning is destroyed, but some holds out bravely, means to persist, *must* persist, making an enclave of meaning in the middle of comparative meaninglessness. Finally, she says that when we can't manage to get meaning into our lives, meaninglessness is accepted as meaning that we don't understand (divine). With this she sums up Masha's and Irina's last lines where they've said "we must live . . ." just as she sums up that half of the play that is meaningful, sensible, and hopeful.

### IRINA

*The endless plain, all alike, without one living soul, frightened her and at moments it was clear to her that this peaceful green vastness would swallow up her life and reduce it to nothingness. She was very young, elegant, fond of life; she had finished her studies at an aristocratic boarding-school, had learnt three languages, had read a great deal, had travelled with her father— and could all this have been meant to lead to nothing but settling down in a remote country house in the steppe, and wandering day after day from the garden into the fields and from the fields into the garden to while away the time, and then sitting at home listening to her grandfather breathing? But what could she do? Where could she go?* He goes on: *It would be nice to become a mechanic, a judge, a commander of a steamer, a scientist; to do something into which she could put all her powers, physical and spiritual and to be tired out and sleep soundly at night. . . .* Further along: *And this constant dissatisfaction with herself and everyone else, this succession of bad mistakes that loom up like a mountain before you whenever you look back on your past, she would accept as her real life, her destiny, and she would expect nothing better. . . . And indeed, there is nothing better! Glorious nature, dreams, music, tell one story, but reality another. Evidently goodness and happiness exist somewhere outside of life.* The story ends: *A month later Vera was living at the iron works.*

*from* At Home, *1897*

PROPERTIES:  White dress, suggestive of a girl's communion dress, wedding dress, or party dress; Italian words, birthday presents, teaching certificate.

HOW SHE MAKES THE PRESENT MEANINGFUL:  By strong family attachments, by planning work, by dreaming of Moscow. (The dream of returning to Moscow is divided among Olga and Andrei and Irina. Olga wants to go back to the good past; Andrei wants to be in the intellectual life of the city; Irina has happy associations with the good past there but mainly anticipates finding the good future: a more beautiful life, work with poetry and with sense, and someone to fall in love with.)

IRINA IS THE AUDIENCE'S OWN YOUTH, hope, beauty, and happiness; and she has their empathy from first to last. In Act I she is surrounded by approvers who keep her sheltered, dependent, and girl-like. What she really wants is for work and love to transform her into a grown-up but, not having gotten this grown-up life yet, she is in a continuation of a child's life with the child's satisfactions gone. The family's staying together is strong in her, and her dreams of Moscow incorporate Olga, Andrei, and Masha, too, "every summer." In the early part of the play Irina wants to keep the family close around her and the brigade close around them. She knows as well as we that, despite her work dream, she is not at all ready to go it alone. Her uneasiness in Act II is apparent whenever she is alone on the stage, and when she says "They've all gone. There's no one left." it is a premonition of her fate in Act IV.

Irina's climax in Act III is in the form of heartbreak and disenchantment. Her stage directions repeatedly tell her to sob and cry. Again, it is significant that, as one of a genteel upbringing as well as the sister closest to Olga's refined sensibilities, Irina is not directed to give way to a loud, hysterical scene in competition

with Natasha's. Her speeches are strong, explicit, and quite moving
when they are not made indistinguishable by high-pitched shouting.
They go well with tears and sobs and, if unhurried, stir the
audience's emotions. When violently played, her lines handicap
our belief in her maturing moment when she decides to marry
the Baron according to Olga's advice. Still clinging to her dream
of Moscow, Irina finishes Act III half grown-up.

Irina, open and enthusiastic, is ideally suited for the crisscrossings
of others' traits. It happens at once with Vershinin whom she
scarcely has anything to do with, really. In his first long philo-
sophical speech he says something about "supposing there are only
three people like you. It's plain that you won't be able to get the
better of the darkness and ignorance around you . . . their life
will choke you." Just minutes after this Irina says to the Baron,
"For us three sisters life hasn't been beautiful, it's choked us the
way weeds choke grass." How delicately we are shown by this that
Irina is an impressionable young girl borrowing big thoughts
from the big ones. What we can't know until we know the end
of the play is that this is the genesis of her serious and final speech
three acts later. After the years have passed and so much happens
to her, she comes to find out for herself what Vershinin meant
by life's being beautiful in the future because of the people who
dream about it now and work for it to happen. When we hear
what she says the second time (in Act IV), it is no longer a girl's
mimicry but a woman's conviction.

Irina and Masha illuminate each other by their contrast. They
are as far apart, of course, as the white of Irina's dress is from the
black of Masha's—as far apart as hope is from despair, as virginity
from adultery, etc. Even their speech rhythms—Irina's legato and
Masha's terse, staccato—differentiate them. And yet, if there were
no other lines in the play but what Irina and Masha say to each
other, we would know these two were sisters just as well as
Chekhov knew he had brothers.

See how the nursery warfare persists! In Act I it is the unhappy,
manless Olga who "understands" Masha's gloominess at the birthday party with "a man and a half" while the happy, plan-making
Irina, full of herself, is unmoved by Masha's depression and even

vexed by her wanting to leave, so that she says (*discontentedly*), "How can you be so . . ." (so full of *your* self on *my* birthday). A year or so later, in Act II, Masha tells Irina (who now has her first grown-up job) how thin she looks, how young and like a little boy. That this is belittling on Masha's part we see from Tuzenbach's mildly defensive, "It's the way she does her hair." Still, in the next sentences Irina and Masha unite against the common enemy, Natasha, and in another minute are laughing together over Chebutykin. The significance is more profound when later in the act Masha displaces her anger (over Vershinin's wife's sending for him) on Anfisa, first, and then Irina. "Let me sit down," she says, and then crossly musses up Irina's game. "Sprawling all over the place with your cards. Drink your tea!" she says. And Irina says, "Masha, you're just mean." And Masha says, "Well, if I'm mean, don't talk to me. Don't bother me!" While Vershinin has caused this explosion, it calls attention to Irina's sexually unawakened state, and Masha couldn't have been more impatient with her if the cards had been dolls she was playing with. This seems to be a reenactment of Irina's incomprehension of Masha's moodiness in Act I, and it is a tightening turn of the key in the machine of Masha's tears-and-depression in Act I which was sexually based then, too.

In Act III, after Vershinin and Masha are in love and Kulygin wanders in with his untimely but touching "My darling Masha, my precious Masha . . ." Irina takes hold in a mature fashion worthy of Olga when she says to him, "She's worn out. . . . Let her rest, Fyodor dear." And in Act IV Irina conspicuously copies Masha's leitmotiv "fate" when she says she is fated not to go to Moscow. Later she has grown so much in sympathy toward Masha and the love affair that it is she, Irina, who volunteers to go and find Masha and bring her to Vershinin to say good-bye.

Irina's arias are the most overwhelming in the play. Work, beauty, belief, happiness are her predominant themes and belong as she does on the side of meaning (what there is in life that has meaning). Her leitmotivs of loneliness and leaving and frustration and forgetting are an interlacing of negative themes from the

side of meaninglessness. Here again, Chekhov is schematically
unschematic and seeking to disguise the actors in order that we
might think they are people.

*The Three Sisters* is not just about a family, it is one; and if an
audience only meets it for an afternoon or an evening, how *can*
it catch all those family jokes and allusions? For instance, we hear
Irina's slightly absurd first speech about work: "A man must
work, must make his bread by the sweat of his brow, no matter
who he is—and it is in this alone that he can find the purpose and
meaning of his life, his happiness, his ecstasies. Oh, how good
it is to be a workman who gets up at dawn and breaks stones
in the street, or a shepherd, or a schoolteacher who teaches children, or a locomotive engineer! My God, it is better to be an
ox, a plain horse, and *work*, than to be a girl who wakes up at
twelve o'clock, has coffee in bed, and then spends two hours
getting dressed." We see that this is spoken to Chebutykin, and
that he listens; but if only we knew—the way the family knows—
what a monument of laziness he is, this would be a small, favorite,
comic bit like something in *The Marriage of Figaro* that audiences
would wait for and smile over.

As it is, though, it has a fine surface success in showing
Chebutykin's best (grandfatherly) side. Our hearts ease about him
when he calls Irina his darling, his "own little girl" whom he's
known from the day of her birth and carried in his own arms.
The affection and companionship between the youngest one and
the oldest one in the family add human warmth and sweetness that
are rooted in the past. It is important to see how much Chebutykin
counts with Irina at this stage, in contradiction to Tuzenbach's
saying to him earlier, "You don't count." Olga and Masha, of
course, have written Chebutykin off as "silly" and "shameless"
and, with their grown-up eyes see his irresponsibility and moral
deterioration. Irina has not (yet), and he is still quite often her
"dear Ivan Romanich."

Upholding all this, invisibly until we look for them, are
Chebutykin's and Irina's parallel phrases. Usually the meanings
are at variance, but the words are duplicates and have the effect
of that phrase "singing the same words to a different tune," i.e.,

Irina's "Life's gone by and won't ever come back" and Chebutykin's
"Life's gone by like lightning," her, "You say life is beautiful.
Yes, but what if it only seems that way?" and his only "seeming"
to exist, to be a man, to break the clock, etc. What is more
truthful and natural than that two people who are used to being
with each other will talk like each other? But what is astonishing
is Chekhov's carrying this to its limits in Act III when, under
catastrophic circumstances, Chebutykin and Irina use many identical
words for their entirely dissimilar revelations.

Chebutykin says, ". . . I've forgotten everything I ever did
know, I remember nothing, absolutely nothing. . . . Last Wednesday
I treated a woman at Zasyp—dead, and it's my fault she's dead.
Yes. . . . Twenty-five years ago I used to know a little something,
but now I don't remember a thing. One single, thing. Maybe
I'm not a man at all, but just look like one. . . . Maybe I don't even
exist, and it only looks like I walk and eat and sleep. (HE *cries*)
Oh, if only I didn't exist!"

And Irina says, "Where's it all gone? . . . I've forgotten
everything, forgotten. . . . I don't remember what *window* is in
Italian, or *ceiling*. . . . I'm forgetting everything." And farther on,
"Everything is getting away from any real life, beautiful life,
everything's going farther and farther into some abyss. . . . I am
in despair, I can't understand how I'm alive, how I haven't killed
myself long ago. . . ." With the same means that Chekhov holds
them together he breaks them in two.

Causally, Irina has not heard Chebutykin's speech and so is not
alienated, specifically, by that. We must infer that simply by
growing up more she sees more and begins to draw away from
him. An intimation of this distance is certainly intended by
having Chebutykin break that clock. Irina is the only one who
comments on it. With one of the shortened speeches she will use
increasingly to him in the last half of the play, she says only,
"That was Mother's clock." With it in "smithereens" and
Chebutykin quite unmoved, there is a diminution of (1) the
material evidence of Mother and the past and (2) Chebutykin's
love for the mother and his position—by this association—of
special family member.

In Act III, joke as he will and sentimentalize as he does—his
protective ambiguities continue to be spectacular—Chebutykin
is not as close to Irina as he formerly was. Or, the reverse:
Chebutykin is the same "incorrigible" person, but Irina is not as
close to him. When he talks of coming back in a year to be near
her and leading a "new life, sober and respectable," Irina's answer
is again in Olga's key, "Yes, you really ought to, my dove.
Somehow or other you ought." Here, his furtiveness about the
duel echoes his "being up to something" about the samovar in
Act I. Irina is packed and ready to marry the Baron and leave the
next day; but at this moment she is uneasy (shivers) and is
remindful of her apprehensiveness in Act II at being left alone.
Accountably she does not answer Chebutykin's speech about her
being "my treasure. . . . My wonderful girl. . . . You have gone
on far ahead, I'll never catch up with you. I'm left behind
like a bird that's too old to fly. . . . etc." Curiously, Irina speaks
to him just once more before the end when he has told Olga
first about the Baron's death in the duel and then tells her. All
that she says is, "I knew, I knew. . . ."

In Act IV Irina has come to the end of her dream of Moscow,
and she, who never used it before, uses Masha's phrase, "It's fate."
In declaring she will marry the Baron, even without love, she
approaches Olga's disinterestedness and grown-up attitudes about
duty. When the Baron is killed in the duel, she has nothing left
of the present but her dream of work. The dream of work *has*
materialized along with her independence of childhood and the
family organization so that she can say ". . . work, only work!
Tomorrow I'll go away alone, I'll teach in the school and give
my life to those who'll need it, perhaps. . . . I will work, I will
work . . ."

She is grown now, but there is a pathos in her (and the
others), necessity for illusions, dreams-are-necessary. Partly we
see this in her last lines; partly we see her courage, the feeling
that even if one hasn't managed to find a meaningfully occupied
life (that is of some use to oneself and the world), one will
try again.

## MASHA

*In the story* My Life *(1896) about another Masha, a talented singer who deserts the hero who—uneasy about her—keeps saying, "Lovely, wonderful Masha. My dear Masha. . . ." Chekhov writes: "And Masha looked as though she had wakened from a long sleep and was astonished to find herself, so clever, so educated, so refined, cast away in this miserable provincial hole, among a lot of petty, shallow people, and to think that she could have so far forgotten herself to have been carried away by one of them and to have been his wife for more than half a year. . . ."*

PROPERTIES: Literary quotations, tears, hat, pillow, whistled phrase, musical phrase for Vershinin, black dress, book, cup, cape and hat.

HOW SHE MAKES THE PRESENT MEANINGFUL: Masha is so *angry* at the complete frustration of her present that she makes it even worse for herself by giving up the piano, hardly talking, not wanting to be with people (even her family), and continuing to wear black after the father's death.

MASHA IS THE MOST FRUSTRATED AND ANGRIEST OF THE SISTERS because she is the most exceptional, intelligent, gifted; a large thing compressed into a small space. She suffers more from the status of women in those days because of her temperament and her abilities. She needs "work" the most but never says a word about it and is absolutely idle. Irina and Olga have suffered in the provincial environment, too, but they sublimate in their dream of Moscow and in beliefs in personal worth. There is a force in Masha: *Accept no substitutes.*

She has the masculine bluntness and strength Andrei lacks. Just as the demands on Andrei are overwhelming, the demands on Masha are insufficient. How sympathetically these lines tell us what she is like:

You really don't know how dull and stupid it is to go to bed
at nine in the evening and lie there in a fury and with the
consciousness that there is nowhere to go, no one to talk to,
and nothing to work for because it makes no difference
what you do if you don't see and hear your work. The piano
and I are the two objects in the house existing mutely, wonder-
ing always why we have been placed here, since there is no
one to play us.

(They are not in the play but from a letter Chekhov wrote
from Yalta to Olga Knipper in Moscow at the same time he
was writing *The Three Sisters*.)

When the play begins Masha sits for a quarter of an act without
saying a word. Then quoting a line of poetry to herself and
humming to herself, she puts on her hat and starts to leave. Her
birthday speech to Irina is a long one for her but breaks into her
own personal terse, staccato rhythms. These make for a peculiar
character type, not as general as Irina's "young girl" and narrower
than Olga's. She hasn't the arias nor leitmotivs of Irina, but
more of an interchanging, intermingling of anger-boredom themes.
These disappear while she is in love and in Act IV are replaced
by sorrow.

Masha wants Moscow as much as Olga and Irina do, but hers
is a different sort. Theirs, and Andrei's (until he takes a wrong
turn just the way Masha did), is a somewhat likely possibility,
something good to look to in the future, and a means of changing
their lives. Because she had cut off her future by her marriage to
Kulygin, Masha could have none of this. At best she could migrate
there in the summers. So, her Moscow is the past with the orderlies
in it, the officers in uniform, who were the "nicest, decentest,
best-mannered people," and high-ranking, trilingual Father overall.
No wonder she wears black with all that gone. She cries because
she is depressed on Irina's birthday, but partly her tears are for the
injustice of her irreparable misfortune.

Masha is the audience's own anger and frustration so far as the
Prozorovs and Natasha are concerned. We want helpless, cultivated Olga and Irina (and Andrei) successfully to resist Natasha
and the Protopopov world. We want the sisters and the brother to

do something for their own happiness. Masha is the only one who does, and we are glad she has the love affair. We accept all her anger, too, as we wouldn't in other circumstances. The other person in the play who has the stage direction (*angrily*) is the other woman of action, Natasha, who keeps fighting-for the way Masha keeps fighting-back.

A human, all-too-human trait Chekhov gives Masha is her repeated displacing of her anger on innocent bystanders. In Act I when Solyony has vexed her about philosophizing women, she answers him sharply and has sufficient residue to say (*angrily*), "Don't sit there sniveling!" to Olga who has just been giving her sympathy! Again in that act, when Kulygin tells her about going to the outing and to the principal's, she answers him, "I'm not going." and in two minutes is (*sternly*) threatening Chebutykin, "Nothing to drink today. Do you hear? . . . Don't you dare!" along with (*angrily*), "Oh damnation, damnation! for another evening to sit and be bored to death at that principal's!" A dazzling example is in Act II when Vershinin is called away to his wife. Masha gets so furious that her anger lands on Anfisa, the old servant, then Irina, the younger sister, and then ricochets off hapless Chebutykin.

Here, Natasha says (*sighs*), "Dear Masha, why must you use such expressions in conversation? . . . Forgive me for mentioning it, Masha, but your manners *are* a little coarse." And what happens to Natasha for this? Nothing. Tuzenbach can hardly keep from laughing at what has happened. But Masha is simply above Natasha and on a different level of being. We know her opinion of Natasha. She could demolish her in one swoop, we feel. Actually she never speaks to her during the whole play!

This seems planned, since Masha is having a love affair just as Natasha is, and a collision between them could become a violent, yelling scene, and all that the play has told us about the enclave's accustomed genteel behavior in contrast to the environment's vulgarity would be undone. This is true also of the Natasha-Prozorov quarrel in Act III when Olga represents the family in shocked low tones. Pitting Masha against her there would again have been too risky.

Being in love represses none of this but adds to Masha what had been suppressed before: animation, gaiety, "life" in place of mourning-for-life. Vershinin and she are two-complainers-about-unhappy-marriages who love Moscow. As soon as she meets him she takes a drink (getting a C-minus in deportment from Kulygin), then goes on to quoting Gogol, waltzing with herself, and behaving in her usual free style, but cheerfully. In Act II her stage directions over and over are "MASHA (*laughing*)." Vershinin is Masha's Moscow: he is a commanding officer as Father was, forty-three years old to her twenty-four-five-six; he makes speeches and, as Kulygin once had, has ideas fresh to her, persuasively beyond her. And Vershinin becomes her happiness. Although he believes "there *is* no happiness" (happiness as a permanently available, God-given right), he is—Masha says he is—the happiness she got "in snatches, in shreds" and then lost.

The enclave criticizes Natasha's actions as anything from petty to ruthless and always as without spiritual cause or feeling. It simply closes ranks around Masha. When Masha is cross, they treat it as one of her depressed times, when she boils inside or feels irritable. Her love affair is not "held up" (even by Kulygin!) but seems viewed as another inevitability, like Andrei's gambling, that the provincial environment is really to blame for.

In Act III Masha has stopped hiding anything. She no longer takes care (Act II) that Kulygin doesn't overhear her and disregards his feelings openly. Her own feelings for Kulygin are dead when her confession of love for Vershinin is made. After that, when she parodies his "satisfied, satisfied, satisfied" with her "bored, bored, bored," it is the corpse's angry first thrust forth three times from the grave.

There is a resuming of her "coarseness" in Act IV when she talks like Marfa, the cook, and tells how she has come to feel about happiness.

Because Kulygin has been so good about the affair, it is going to be worse for Masha after the play ends. She can still feel intellectually and aesthetically superior to him, but not morally. That her dull, wooden pedant was so "good" makes relations with him impossible. Her speech at the last is much the shortest, which is a partial resuming of her terse speeches in Act I but also is significant in that she is morally the least imposing of the sisters, having expressed her frustration in action as the other two have not.

Thoughts and words she learned from Vershinin survive in her lines throughout Act IV. His doctrines—that there is no happiness now but only work so that happiness and progress will come in the future, and, that it *does* matter to have existed—exist in her ". . . we'll stay here alone, to begin our life again. We must live . . . we must live . . ." has, as last, a hint of reconciling in it. Different from Olga's and Irina's ". . . we shall live," Masha's says we must manage to get satisfaction out of what we tried before to avoid as unsatisfactory.

### ANDREI

*When you dream of playing a part, of becoming known, of being, for instance, examining magistrate in important cases or prosecutor in a circuit court, ("a famous scholar of whom all Russia is proud"), you inevitably think of Moscow; here nothing matters to you; you get reconciled readily enough to your insignificant role, and only look for one thing in life—to get away, to get away as quickly as possible. And in his mind Lyzhin hurried through the Moscow streets, called on acquaintances, met relatives, colleagues, and his heart contracted sweetly at the thought that he was only twenty-six, and that in five or ten years he could break away from here and get to Moscow, even then, it would not be too late and he would still have a whole life ahead of him.*

*from* ON OFFICIAL BUSINESS, *1899*

PROPERTIES:   Violin, fretsaw, English book to translate, candle and book, papers to sign, Ferapont, key to cupboard, baby carriage, cottage cheese, cards, mortgage.

HOW HE MAKES THE PRESENT MEANINGFUL:   By playing the violin, fretsawing, dreaming of translating a book from English, dreaming of being a professor at Moscow University, dreaming

of being in Moscow, reading, gambling, dreaming of the future.
By soliloquizing. *When they tell you there are lots of remedies
for a disease, it's incurable.*

ANDREI HAS A SENSITIVE, SWEET THOUGH COMMONPLACE NATURE
that had too great demands on it by the Father. Now, the sisters
more or less expect Andrei, as a man, to do what they as women
are not allowed to do (carry on where Father left off) and what
Andrei is too weak to do. In Act I when the sisters introduce
Andrei to the new battery commander from Moscow as "our
scholar" and a "universal expert," he sweats and has to wipe his
face and wants to be let alone. Though he reads and does mention
translating a book from English, he never makes literary remarks
or even "scholarly" ones. It turns out the plan for Andrei to be
a professor was really Father's idea; and it soon stops being a plan
and turns into a dream. During the speech in which Vershinin
talks about the importance of the cultivated individual (when
Masha takes off her hat and says, "I'm staying to lunch."),
Andrei walks off!

The truth is, in Act I, Andrei is a joke about a violin, a fretsaw,
and one of the local girls. He's a joke that has gone on in some
form as part of a harmless, and not so harmless, three-against-one
game that began in kindergarten or before, and that "Andrei
is always going off by himself" to get away from. And yet,
Andrei is a Prozorov as much as the sisters, the weakest Prozorov,
but part of what they are part of and included with them—and
by them—in the plan to go to Moscow.

When he tells Natasha not to mind the teasing, he says, ". . . they
mean well. They have such kind hearts—my darling . . . They're
all such kind-hearted people, they love both of us. . . ." We
know Andrei has had kindness and love in this family, and he is
on that side of things that is against rudeness and cruelty. In his
rapturous proposal he dreams, and we dream with him, that it
will be as he says in his marriage. Instead, we are all slapped in
the face by Act II. He'd sought refuge in Natasha from the others
who made him feel lonely and shy; then, Natasha becomes the
worst of all. Then he seeks refuge in poor, deaf old Ferapont, who

wouldn't object, tease, make Andrei feel inferior, even if he could hear, and he can't hear.

Andrei is a loneliness figure—lonely with people and lonely without them. He tells his feelings in long soliloquies to deaf Ferapont and to his only friend, the unvaluing, newspaper-reading, "What's the difference?" Chebutykin. (Who can feel inferior to Chebutykin?) This eccentric uncle figure who loved the mother and has always been around the family is in no way a forbidding father figure and is the logical friend for Andrei—worthless enough to excuse one's own worthlessness.

Andrei doesn't put "If only" into words so that it becomes a noticeably pervading theme in the play, as the others have. ("If only I were married"—Olga. "If only I worked"—Irina. "If only this life were a rough draft"—Vershinin. "If only I didn't exist"— Chebutykin. Etc.) But Chekhov makes him the personification of these words, and by intuition we come to know Andrei on one level by his: "*If only* I were married to Natasha; *If only* I weren't married to Natasha; *If only* I were in Moscow at the University; *If only* they understood me, didn't make fun of me; *If only* I were young again; *If only* it were the future;—Really, *if only everything were different!*"

While in Act II Andrei's relations with Ferapont are kind and sympathetic, Act III starts with a nervous Andrei, unable to meet even Ferapont's demands. Instead of calling him "Ferapont, old man" in friendship with an inferior, Andrei insists that Ferapont make his inferior status plain by calling the county board member "your honor." This is a frightening litmus-paper indication of Andrei's own depreciation. As Irina says, "How petty our Andrei's become . . . at the side of that woman."

Our bad expectations about Andrei build up in Act III with the gambling debts, the underhanded mortgaging of the house (he is too cowardly to talk it over with the sisters first), and the boasting of his appointment to the county board by his wife's lover. During the fire he does nothing to help either the men fighting it or the women assisting the victims, and remains in his room playing his violin. In this act the distance between the three sisters and Andrei becomes great. Teasing and overexpectant as they were with him formerly, still he was "our brother" and they had an affectionate trust that he'd turn out all right in the long run. It is different, now. Irina and Masha have talked about his gambling losses and his general decline. Olga has been silent toward him. Andrei is well aware of their disapproval, their justified disapproval. When he does rise up in his own behalf and Natasha's, they evade any discussion with him. "Let it go now, Andrei dear," Olga says. "We'll settle things tomorrow." But what is left to settle? Andrei's weak nature, indecisiveness, and his real incapacity to use the present are taking on a certain shape the sisters have seen before—they know it well—the shape of indifference, unconcern, and undeniable laziness that resembles Chebutykin more every day. He even sentimentalizes, like Chebutykin, "My dearest sisters, darling sisters, don't believe me . . ." in Act III, and again in Act IV, "My own darling sisters, my wonderful sisters . . ." Just as they have given up on Chebutykin, they have relinquished all the hopes for Andrei— and Andrei knows it.

Act IV is a study in abjectness. It begins with Andrei at his humbling task of pushing the baby carriage. Masha sets the tone with her speech about the bell, raised at such cost, that falls and breaks. That Andrei is like such a bell seems right, but her "for no reason at all" seems a little hard on him. Or does it?

He does raise himself a millimeter above Chebutykin when he says, "In my opinion, to take part in a duel, to be present at one, even in the capacity of doctor, is simply immoral." But he will not act. Andrei has sat through his days "sawing away" while his plans turned to dreams and his dreams faded. Now he just has words: soliloquies. His present is proven as meaninglessly lived as Chebutykin's, but he hasn't found Chebutykin's trick of nihilism. He is still back in the dream stage, the childlike "if only" stage. In his last soliloquy he does admit the difference between the Prozorov past and the Protopopov world of the present, but absurdly dreams that the future will somehow clear away all the "laziness, vodka, goose and cabbage, naps after dinner, cowardice" that is Andrei's existence. He no longer makes any case for

Natasha. He knows now that she is an animal; but he knows, too, that he is the one in the trap.

The sisters are leaving, Chebutykin is leaving; Andrei says, "I'll be the only one left," wishfully forgetting Natasha, just as she later says, "Tomorrow I'll be all alone here." quite forgetting him. In these last minutes Andrei is reduced to someone interchangeable with Ferapont to push babies. After Natasha reprimands him for talking too loudly, Andrei speaks in a low voice and signs the papers. He has no further word, just pushes the baby carriage. This cynical, almost brutal wiping-out of Andrei is as final as ending up in the family graveyard, where, as Astroff says, late in *Uncle Vanya*, "There's but one hope for you and me. The hope that when we'll be sleeping in our coffins, we might be visited by dreams, perhaps even pleasant ones." A few dreams visiting the completely defeated, utterly abject Andrei are the only remnant of the enclave's strong father, cultivated sisters, and weary, once dutiful brother.

## CHEBUTYKIN

*But now nothing mattered to him anymore. He neither ate nor drank, but lay motionless and silent on his bed. "It's all the same," he thought, when they asked him questions. "I shan't answer. . . . It's all the same."*

*from* WARD NO. 6, *1892*

PROPERTIES: Newspaper, random quotations, samovar, drinking, knocking on floor, washing hands, combing beard, notebook, old-fashioned watch, speeches, jokes, "always doing something silly," walking stick, "What's the difference?" The devil is a "property" Chebutykin calls upon in his speeches from time to time, and this characteristic is contrasted with the others' calling upon God in their speech.

HOW HE MAKES LIFE MEANINGFUL: He doesn't. He finds the present meaningless, just as Masha has begun to and Andrei will later on. He philosophizes that "meaning" is impossible, and this theme is remindful of Vershinin's "happiness is impossible" but, of course, is more extreme and sinister.

THERE IS A COMIC WORTHLESSNESS ABOUT CHEBUTYKIN that the enclave takes for granted, along with his oddness, and the fact that there is something wrong with him, and that he does such "stupid, silly things." Insofar as he stands for nondreams, nonwork, nonevaluation, nonexistence, Chebutykin is a one-character Theater of the Absurd; and his two newspapers are a perfect symbol of his being distracted from distraction by distraction.

In the play, Chebutykin represents the complete devaluation of values. "What's the difference?" is his personal leitmotiv and also a general leitmotiv standing for meaninglessness, senselessness, and hopelessness that, now and then, infects the others. For him, it is the way he has managed to reconcile himself to existing: "What's the difference?" equates everything. As the play progresses, he repeats it more and more until we see it *is* a piece of dramatic organization Chekhov means us to be conscious of.

"What's the difference?" "It doesn't make any difference." is people's regular desperate denial—the more difference it makes, the more surely they say, "It makes no difference." to try to cheer themselves up, to bridge the awful gap between what they want and what they get. (It is worth noticing the climaxes of one kind or another that provoke this phrase from each of the sisters, Andrei, Tuzenbach, Vershinin, and Solyony.)

Chebutykin's forgetting goes right along with "What's the difference?" It is his further breaking down of values and the good system of things, and is his way out of being responsible for his acts. An extraordinary example of this is his answer to Andrei about what to do for asthma: "Why ask me?" he says. "I don't remember, Andrei boy. I don't know." And consider his "I don't remember . . ." when Masha asks if her mother loved him.

In Acts I, II, and IV his nonremembrance and nonemotion protect him from intolerable guilt, but in climactic Act III Chebutykin has his last flurry of normal attitudes. He reveals a worse thing about himself than we could have suspected, in that he is actually to blame for the death of his woman patient the week before. And then a rather touching confession about his (and the others') "cheap low pretense" at the club that, coming on top of the first and real and terrible cause of his miserableness, makes him "feel inside all twisted, all vile, all nauseating. . . ." These are the last manifestations of full humanity in him and the very opposite of "What's the difference?" Here Chebutykin borrows the leitmotiv "If only" from the hopeful, life-does-have-meaning side, in his longing, weeping, "If only I didn't exist!" Here he acknowledges that there *is* so much difference between what is good and what is bad in human existence that he is unable to pretend that there is none, and wishes for the nonexistence in which there is no difference between nothing and nothing.

In Act IV, in both his words and actions, Chebutykin has recovered his equanimity. He again takes refuge, as he formerly did, in saying, no matter what happens, "What's the difference?" Three out of four speeches consist of this concentrated essence of Chebutykin: the disgusted, helpless assertion of the meaning-lessness of existence.

Tuzenbach is dead and Irina and her sisters weep for him, and Chebutykin (who has indifferently let the Baron die) exclaims, "The Baron's a good man, but one baron more, one baron less—what's the difference?" He then concludes his part of the play by twice singing his trivial, complacent theme song of the fourth act, "Ta-ra-ra-boom-de-aye . . . / Sit on a log, I may . . ." and by three times repeating "What's the difference, anyway?" From his breakdown in Act III, though, we know that this is as much of a denial as Kulygin's thrice-stated "I'm satisfied."

## VERSHININ

*Those who will live a hundred, two hundred years after us and who will despise us because we have lived our lives so stupidly and so without any taste—Those, perhaps, will find the way how to be happy.*

*Astroff*: Uncle Vanya (*1899*)

PROPERTIES:    Uniform, wife and daughters, letter.

HOW HE MAKES LIFE MEANINGFUL:    By philosophizing about the future. Saying to himself and others that the present is necessarily *meaningless* except as an interim: a bad prelude to a good future. This is Vershinin's "theme," his "Vuillard spot," and his one, long, four-act aria.

VERSHININ'S PHILOSOPHIZING IS A PLAUSIBLE EXCUSE for Chekhov to have much talk about ultimates. But, actually, when people are unhappy, frustrated, trying to justify a bad existence, or made to question something that goes against them, they *do* talk about ultimates and the meaning of life. When people are happy, they forget to.

Vershinin's many big speeches of imaginative, well-phrased philosophizing make his surface show up well, and his more troubling depths have to be inferred. He does have them, of course. Think of telling people the first time one meets them, "I often think if it were possible to begin life over again . . . If only the first life . . . were a rough draft . . . I believe that each of us would try above all not to repeat himself—or at least would create a different set of circumstances for his life, would manage to live in a house like this, with flowers, with plenty of light . . . Well, if I could begin life over again, I'd never get married. . . . Never, never!" Naturally, we infer, as Masha does, that he's given up on love and personal happiness. "If only I could make you see that there *is* no happiness, that there should not be, and that there will not be, for us." Although Tuzenbach and Masha then defend happiness, Vershinin is unmoved and says more firmly than ever, "We aren't happy, we never will be, we only long to be." This is the life Vershinin lives, instead of the life he dreams of; that is to say, the frustrations we reconcile ourselves to, this is the life Vershinin lives. It is a life going on year after year that is partly starved, keeps wanting (as in Act II) a cup of tea— just a little cup of tea—that it doesn't ever get.

We see the most of Vershinin in the first half of the play, and his main change is between Act I and Act II. He is excited by the new acquaintances and this new place that seems better to him than Moscow, so that he is affable in his early speeches, and his spirits are up in Act I (just the reverse of Masha) and come down in Act II (as hers rise). There is a charming interplay between his enthusiasm for the enclave (the Prozorov establishment just the way it is) and the three sisters' enthusiasm for him as a Moscow substitute. They are novelties for each other, each admiring the other's weather and situation and depreciating his own. The "gloomy bridge" that the lonely man feels melancholy about, and, of course, the big speech about living life over again, imply that being lonely is Vershinin's regular state that the excitement of the moment has overshadowed.

His wanting to come again that evening, his saying, "I feel so good here at your house!" show a touching eagerness to be adopted by this home away from home. He immediately links himself to the three sisters, but *not* to Andrei. Notice that Vershinin can't summon up the least conventional empty compliment for poor Andrei's poor picture frame. And when Masha says to Andrei that Vershinin was never angry when teased about being the love-sick major, "never angry, not even once," Vershinin cheerfully repeats, "Not even once," making himself part of the girls' teasing, especially Masha's, instead of coming to Andrei's defense with even a mild "Well, I did used to get annoyed sometimes, etc." This completely identifies him with the superior three sisters. Vershinin never acts as if their brother were their equal. In his speech about the need for intelligent people (however few there are) among the hundred thousand inhabitants of this "obviously crude, obviously backward place," he says, "Suppose there are only three people like you?" Why doesn't he say four? Poor, weak Andrei.

Of course, the small, superior enclave itself, in the midst of the inferior present, is ideal for Vershinin's philosophy of the beautiful future to come. Simply by existing, being defeated and choked out, it magically makes the future. His belief that cultivation can multiply, that industry and education will—in time—make secular progress for mankind, is Vershinin's religion substitute and parallels Olga's belief that in the future man will make spiritual progress. These are Chekhov's personal views that Vershinin holds, and

he also gave them to Astroff in *Uncle Vanya*. That Chekhov was
entirely serious about them is shown in a letter to Diaghilev in
1902:

> Modern culture is only the beginning of an effort in the name
> of a great future, an effort that will continue perhaps for
> tens of thousands of years, in order that humanity, if only in
> the remote future, may come to know the truth of the real God,
> that is, not guess at it or seek it in Dostoevsky, but know it
> just as clearly as we know that twice two is four.

Act I is a vivacious novelty for Vershinin, but Act II is bored
habit so far as the town is concerned. All the intellectuals seem
equally uninteresting to him. He's depressed and talks about
Russians who have such lofty ideals but low aims, about Russian
husbands who are sick and tired of their wives and children, and
about their wives and children who are sick and tired of them.

He has fallen in love with Masha, and in Act III he says, "I want
like the devil to live." He has found in love something to sing
about, and he and Masha sing snatches of song back and forth
to each other in the midst of the hubbub of the fire and in the
crises in the other lives around them. But how love affects him—
other than this—we don't see. He makes no revelation about
himself in Act III as the others do. Is there nothing to reveal? Or
is there something held back that no one fully knows? Vershinin
seems an incomplete character whom Chekhov made that way
to simulate an incomplete person. We get some idea of what
Vershinin is like from what Masha says about him: "At first he
seemed strange to me, then I felt sorry for him . . . then I fell in
love with him, fell in love with his voice, his words, his misfortunes." He is primarily someone who speaks beautifully. He reads
and then likes to think and talk about what he's read; also, though,
as Tuzenbach said in the beginning, "He goes around calling on
people and telling them he has a wife and two little girls. He'll
tell you that." Yes, he has fallen in love with Masha, although
how much can you be in love if you believe happiness is
impossible? We have to believe love brings us happiness (and
Masha believed this) if we thoroughly believe in love.

In Chekhov's story *Three Years* (1895) the character Laeptev says, "All hopes of personal happiness must be left behind and one must live without desires, without hopes, not dreaming, not expecting, and to avoid this boredom one was already tired of cultivating, one could become interested in others' affairs, others' happiness, and age would come on imperceptibly, life would come to an end—and nothing more was necessary." This might very well be Vershinin's course after he leaves the Prozorovs.

<br>

## KULYGIN

*To see and hear how they lie . . . endure insult, humiliation . . . and to lie and smile . . . all for a crust of bread, for the sake of a warm corner, for some lowly rank in the service [teaching] that is not worth a farthing . . .*

*from* THE MAN IN THE SHELL, *1897*

PROPERTIES:  Notebooks, Latin quotations, uniform, shaved-off moustache, grades, numbers, jokes, Order of Stanislaus, false moustache, the institution of marriage.

HOW HE MAKES THE PRESENT MEANINGFUL: By work, by looking up to the principal, by being good to Masha, by sticking to routine, by denying unhappiness.

KULYGIN IS A SIMPLE, LOWER-LEVEL ORGANISM with a lower-level expectation in life. The side of Kulygin that bores Masha is his repetitive, routinized, wooden specificness. He is the only one in the play who consistently utters numerical expressions: "Your clock is seven minutes fast," "Thirteen at table," "I worked until eleven," "Everyone who graduated from the high school in fifty years," "At four o'clock we go to the principal's." Persons of this kind often enunciate with particular clarity, and their t's and s's are exaggerated.

His jokey and good-humored side goes along with his timidity— if I joke and am willing to seem absurd, they won't hurt me; nor do I want to hurt them. (This is a point of interest when we

compare how Kulygin has made *use* of being laughed at with
Andrei's being so injured by it.) He is almost psychotic about
avoiding trouble, scenes, and anger; this is one of his strong leit-
motivs that is echoed faintly but surely in Olga's "We'll talk
tomorrow. . . . We'll settle things later." and in her response to
Masha's confession: "I don't hear what silly things you are saying."
Superficially these seem mostly due to Kulygin's timidity and
Olga's refined sensitivities; but—as we have come to expect—
Chekhov is asserting that there are varying amounts of both
these qualities in both characters.

Another refuge for Kulygin is routine. When he quotes the
principal's "That which loses its routine, loses its existence," he's
told us a great deal about himself. We see why, having found the
routine of Latin declensions, academic life, and the institution
of marriage, he cannot break away from any of them. Routine,
being the opposite of chaos to Kulygin, must be preserved, and
any threat to routine he denies. How terribly dissatisfied a man
must be to need to repeat so often: "I'm satisfied, I'm satisfied,
I'm satisfied." Doesn't it sound much more as if it took three
pushes to push down all his resentment and dissatisfaction? His
denial, denial, denial is like Hopkins' "Not, I'll not, carrion comfort,/Despair, not feast on thee; . . ." Kulygin is so frightened
of any admission of aggression that in the earlier acts he constantly
says Masha's disposition is good (!) and that she is a wonderful
wife. In Act III when Masha wants to send him home and be
rid of him, he suppresses his resentment saying, "I'll go in just a
minute. My good and wonderful wife . . . I love you." This is
a mixture of saying what isn't so, along with saying that she is his
superior, better than he, and he's lucky to have her. His "I love
you" is true enough, but it is said to damp out, not to admit the
existence of, his legitimate distress. If I always say *I love you,*
you won't hurt me. The more uneasy Kulygin becomes about
Masha, the more he says, "I love you" until it becomes like the
wistful appeal of a wooden cuckoo clock repeating itself every
hour. It is, of course, Kulygin's peculiar way of saying I don't
resent, I haven't changed (about our marriage) even though you
have. I'm giving you the opportunity to change back simply by

saying, "I love you, too" ("I love you" after all does expect an
answering "I love you, too.") Masha's "*Amo, amas, amat*, etc." is
so terribly witty because it displays—even to him—the wooden,
pigeonholed, repetitive, pedantic, occupational deformation of
*his* nature.

Kulygin is half-ridiculous and partially like Belikov, who taught
Greek in the story *The Man in the Shell* (1897) and about whom
Chekhov wrote: "To see and hear how they lie . . . endure insult,
humiliation . . . and to lie and smile . . . all for a crust of bread,
for the sake of a warm corner, for some lowly rank in the
service [teaching] that is not worth a farthing . . ." The difference between them, and this must be stressed when the lines call
for it, is Kulygin's *kindness*. This kindness—a human trait
Chekhov treats with warmth and respect in all his writings—
actually strengthens the absurd side of Kulygin. Against a background of kindheartedness, the humor can stand out and be funnier
than if he were made an unrelievedly foolish figure.

Irina gives us the seed of this in her sentence to Vershinin about
Kulygin, "He is the kindest of men, but not the most intelligent."
Then in Act III when the sisters have been "wronged" by
Andrei's mortgaging their house for gambling debts, all are
condemning Andrei but Kulygin. He knows that what Andrei is
doing is wrong. Although Kulygin has been giving people
C-minuses and zeros on their deportment earlier in the play,
when real morality is at stake, he doesn't judge Andrei (nor later,
Masha). Masha has just said that Andrei is not a decent person
and that what he has done is revolting. In one of the few sentences
in which Kulygin dares to disagree with her, he says, "Must you,
Masha? What's it to you? Poor Andrei's in debt to everybody—
well, God help him." This scene is a preliminary glimpse of how
he is to act in the important scene with Masha. Without being
shown in this earlier scene Kulygin's generosity of nature to
Andrei (who was no threat to him), the audience could have
ambiguous responses to the later one. Knowing Kulygin's timidity,
we could interpret his tolerance of her behavior as "going along"
with the situation out of fear to do otherwise. It is allowable
to think of this as some of his motivation, but mainly Chekhov

wants us, and wants Masha, to credit him for showing her the forbearance that he showed Andrei. Sometimes this small, serious trait of kindness in Kulygin is lost under the avalanche of absurd ones he has. But the more we reread the play, the more apparent is Chekhov's systematic concern with this, and the many other contradictory, uncalled-for, unstereotyped means he uses to mitigate the well-made, pen-and-paper, intellectualized type of character. The most human of characteristics is, after all, something blurred, left undefined, or hazy that, just when we think we have typed a person, puzzles us.

Chekhov's consistency is further borne out by forcing Kulygin to witness Masha's grief and tears at Vershinin's departure (to make certain he can't deny this situation). Then, the stage direction for him is: (*Embarrassed*). What he says to her is, "It's all right, let her cry, let her. . . . My good Masha, my sweet Masha. . . . You're my wife, and I'm happy, no matter what happens. . . . I don't complain, I don't reproach you for a single thing. There's Olga, she'll be our witness. . . . Let's start over and live the way we used to, and I won't by so much as a single word, by the least hint . . ." This speech shows him capable of meeting reality with real decisions when he can't do otherwise. When he accepts something less than ideal, it is because he is constituted to be able to do this. Then, how immediately he seeks out his old comfort, i.e., the joke (moustache joke) that makes Olga laugh and makes Masha, too, stop crying long enough to agree about. Soon, Masha is somewhat recovered and able to talk of going home, and Kulygin's instant obligingness about getting her hat and cape proves him as satisfied as he needs to be about his present.

Earlier in Act IV, before the incontestable truth about Masha and Vershinin is exposed to him, we witness Kulygin's successful adjustment to his worst fears. Justified and logical as it is to resent his situation, he embarks on his long anecdote about "*ut consecutivum*." Being germane to his Latin-academic routines gives him such comfort that it keeps him from allowing himself to express resentment or give in to the wreck of his marriage. Instead, he actually says (compared to "*ut consecutivum*") that he's been lucky

all his life, and that he's happy, and that he's even gotten the
Order of Stanislaus Second Class. That this can cheer him up for
his private failure with Masha, and permit him to pour his heart
into his public success, and constitute his happiness, is touching; but
we believe it, we believe it, we believe it.


TUZENBACH

*See that tree, it's dried up, but the wind moves it with the
others just the same. So it seems to me that if I die, still some
way or other I'll have a share in life. Goodbye, darling. . . .*

TUZENBACH, *Act IV*

PROPERTIES:   German name and Orthodox faith; aristocratic, cultivated St. Petersburg background. Guitar, piano, songs; knowledge of serious music. Cognac (instead of vodka). Uniform,
stylish civilian clothes.

HOW HE MAKES LIFE MEANINGFUL:   By responding to beauty in
music, Irina, nature. By wanting "to share in life," to work with
workers, to attend the University with Andrei, to arrange
the concert to help the fire victims, to marry Irina. By being
good-humored, "decent," believing he is happy, and not
demanding answers about the meaning of life.

TUZENBACH IS THE MASCULINE COUNTERPART of Olga's moral
superiority and the masculine counterpart, too, of Irina's delicacy,
tenderness, and expectancy about life. This links him to those
two more than to any others in the play. Indeed, being as cultivated
and refined, himself, as the three sisters, he is on as close and
comfortable terms with the family as Chebutykin and Kulygin.
   Born under a brighter star, Tuzenbach would have been born
handsome and not ". . . so homely . . . I absolutely wanted to cry,"
as Olga says; and Irina would have been able to marry him for
love and not for duty, as she finally concedes to do. As it is, they
share similar backgrounds and temperaments, they are united
in their goals, and Chekhov has given them all the lyric speeches

in the play. Many of these are extraordinarily beautiful—and
Tuzenbach's are often profound.

When *special care* is taken to have Tuzenbach immediately
recognizable as a homely man, his decisions, his devotion to Irina,
his managing to be happy, and his death all gain interest. He is
an ugly Lensky and when the audience, too, cannot find it in
their "power to love" the honorable, tragic Baron, their sympathy
mounts with their guilt. The "homeliness" that he alludes to once,
and Olga twice, is the one unfavorable quality Chekhov gave
him to counterbalance all his virtues. It is what his whole part
turns on, and if a merely commonplace-looking Tuzenbach is used,
his decisions to resign from aristocratic, wealthy St. Petersburg
first, and then the Army, seem foolhardy; his devotion to Irina,
doglike; his happiness, a simpleton's; his death, as Chebutykin
characterizes it, ". . . one baron more, one baron less—what's
the difference?"

Interpretations that make Tuzenbach ridiculous or comic, i.e.,
stuttering or lisping or lower-class, are not justified in the text. He
should simply have the sort of face that is kind but ugly and
that cancels him out as unattractive to women, because all his
actions are just the reverse.

Now, when an obviously unfortunate-looking man casts away
his birthright and status to work among laborers; when he can
dream that a beautiful girl like Irina—everyone's darling—can
love *him*; when he can believe that constancy and honor are
enough; and when, in spite of being the physical opposite of all
his aesthetic tastes, such a man manages to think of himself as
"happy," we are intrigued. Aren't we?

When such a person says to Irina the ethereal (and perfect for
her) lines about "You're so pale and beautiful and enchanting. . . .
It seems to me your paleness brightens the dark air like light,"
we infer our own "If only . . ." for Tuzenbach. In direct ratio
to his appearance will be the audience's despair at Irina's conceding
to marry him—and soon, the audience's admiration of her spiritual
growth.

Of interest in Act IV are Tuzenbach's only complaining lines

in the play, when he says, "What senseless things, what idiotic
things, suddenly for no reason start to matter in your life! . . ."—
the "senseless things" being an imminent duel and an imminent
marriage to a woman who has told him it is not in her power to
love him. (Chekhov, in an advanced stage of tuberculosis, wrote
Olga Knipper before he went to Moscow to join her, that everything was at last in order for their marriage, "except one trifle
. . . my health.")

When Irina cries and tells him so passionately, "Oh, what is
there I can do? I never have been in love in my life, not even
once. . . . I've dreamed so about love so long now, day and night,
but my soul is like some expensive piano that's locked and the key
is lost." We are moved, and the Baron rises even higher in our
esteem when he tells her, ". . . There isn't anything in my life
terrible enough to frighten me, only that lost key, it tortures
me. . . ."

His saying, "Say something to me" seems at one instant to be
asking for so little and so much. And the real distance between
them is so plain in her "What is there to say?" Still, Tuzenbach's
hope dies hard, it would seem, when he turns back to her, after
starting off for the duel, and calls her name. If only she'd had it
in her power to call him back, or say anything except that blunt
"What?" All he can do is invent a request for some coffee.

### SOLYONY

*Gentlemen, who remembers the description in Lermontov?*
*from* THE DUEL, *1891*

PROPERTIES:  Perfume, literary quotations, resemblance to Lermontov.

HOW HE MAKES LIFE MEANINGFUL:  By looking like and behaving
like and pretending to be Lermontov (the worldly, unscrupulous,
malevolent "friend" of Lensky who takes his fiancée, kills
Lensky in a duel, and then abandons the girl).

Solyony is a menacingly aggressive, antisocial, intellectual man who is shy, panicky, and jealous inside when he is with people. As he says about himself, "When I'm alone with anybody I'm all right, I'm just like everybody else, but . . ." He demands Tuzenbach's entire attention, just as he devours all the candy. He probably falls in love with Irina (inasmuch as his type is able to) because of Tuzenbach. Chekhov convinces us again and again of Solyony's infantile insatiability and pushing of every relation to its limits.

Through his identification with Lermontov, Solyony's inferior, young loneliness is converted (in his imagination) to superior, artistic loneliness. There is in this a curious partial resemblance to Masha in that he always sits by himself, thinking about something and saying nothing. However, Masha's superior, artistic loneliness is true, while his is false; and her anger is against fate, and his is sadism. When Masha speaks, she relates; Solyony erupts with aggressive remarks designed to attract attention, i.e., his first line: "With one hand I can only lift sixty pounds, but with two hands I can lift a hundred and eighty—two hundred, even. From that I deduce, etc. . . ."

He is a great source of bizarre, grotesque texture for the play. Whereas Chekhov presented Olga and Irina to us through their arias (Moscow, work, marriage, etc.) and through the Wagnerian style of leitmotivs, Solyony got none of these. Instead, Chekhov has covered him with little systems of oddness all connetced by their carefully chosen "rightness" for him. Chebutykin and Kulygin are highly specific types, too, who have these Vuillard spots, but Solyony is the concentrated example. His spots range from crude, awkward, childish sentences: "Chicky, chicky, chicky" and "Cockroaches" and others; upward to his spontaneous but heavily aggressive "joke" to Chebutykin that warns us of the duel: "In two or three years either you'll die of apoplexy or I'll lose control of myself and put a bullet through your head, my angel." And on up the scale to the self-revealing misquotation of Lermontov in Act IV, when he says, ". . . Remember the poem? 'But he, the rebel, seeks the storm/ As if in tempests there were peace . . .'"

Solyony hardly has a speech that is not grotesque, and Irina
and Olga haven't a single one that is. His remarks, usually lumped
by the others into "stupidities," are often wit manqué and wit.
He, alone, gets the better of Natasha. Solyony's sentence, "If
that child were mine, I'd fry him in a frying pan and then eat
him," so unexpectedly, grotesquely expresses our own dislike of
Natasha that we laugh and our sympathy is all on his side; and
it is again later, when Natasha is trying for propriety and says,
"Excuse me, Vasili Vasilich, I hadn't any idea you were in here.
I'm not dressed," and he says, "It doesn't make any difference
to me."

Tuzenbach—his complete opposite—is the only person Solyony
feels close to, or comfortable with, and feels safe in his aggression
toward, which, oddly, is partly an expression of affection. His
mildest hostility is in his sentence about vodka's being made
of cockroaches, with which he shocks Irina like a little boy showing
a little girl a live spider. The duel, of course, is the carrying to
the limit of this same impulse. It is thoroughly adult behavior
in which he feels none of his usual adolescent or childish lacks.
On the day of the duel he feels not simply *like* Lermontov; he
feels that for once, he *is* Lermontov.

Solyony is victorious, but he sits among graves. Tuzenbach is
gone, Irina going. The third duel for Solyony is not apt to be
his last. We can imagine him reduced to soldier's rank finally,
with his isolation complete. Solyony's quarrelsomely leaving the
room in anger and frustration to be alone is a good symbol for
his whole life. He walks out on humanity and kills off his last
echo of a connection with it.

## NATASHA

PROPERTIES: Green belt, Andrei, babies, things about babies, the
rooms, the fork, the candles, nightgown, Protopopov's troika,
the servants, the forks, the trees.

HOW SHE MAKES LIFE MEANINGFUL: The present is entirely
meaningful to Natasha as the base she works on. Her dreams

are not ideals but direct preludes to action—get a better room for the baby, drive out the sisters, get rid of the trees. She is a woman of action whose whole life is a complete animal success and human failure.

NATASHA HAS THE IMPLACABLENESS, SINGLE-MINDEDNESS, AND DE-STRUCTIVE SUCCESS of the animal shrew. (How interesting that we use the same word for such a woman and a little animal that kills and kills insensately. How much unconscious, or implied, knowledge of this type is in our name for it.)

She is not only a type, but a new, created-by-Chekhov type: the female human animal. She is so like many women—the essence of many—that we not only recognize but can't believe she didn't exist before. She has the funniness of a monster, yet everyone realizes so well that she is entirely without self-knowledge, and she is an absurd success. Her type is worthy of Molière or Cervantes and is akin, of course, to such wives in folk tales, yet purely invented by Chekhov. Natasha to herself is good and right, since she has no disinterestedness and can never compare her actions and another's as if hers were another's. She is entirely reasonable, with all humor, sentiment, and human feeling lacking, and is worthy of a war machine in the Department of Defense.

In Act I we see her in an unfamiliar, overawing situation in the society of the cultivated enclave. She says, "I'm just not accustomed to being in—" But how quickly in Act II and to the end the Prozorov household stops being "society" and becomes merely the niche, the habitat of this successful animal! Natasha's completely victorious "What do we have to have that old woman for, too? What for?" makes us see (as is intimated in dozens of other ways) that all human kindness, decency, immemorial tradition, "She's been with us thirty years," are helpless against Natasha. If others are ineffective because of distance, uncertainty, she is completely effective because of her lack of any distance, uncertainty—as effective and sure as a wolverine, shrew. To keep Anfisa and take care of her, Olga *must* move to the government apartment at the high school.

Just as Olga is elementally incomprehensible to Natasha, Olga's counterpart, the Baron, is lost on Natasha, too. Compare what he says about the trees, "I'm happy. It's as if I were seeing for the first time in my life these firs and maples and birches, and they are all looking at me curiously and waiting. What beautiful trees, and how beautiful life ought to be under them!" with Natasha's "Tomorrow I'll be all alone here," (mentally she's rid of Andrei, too) "First of all, I'm going to have them chop down all those fir trees along the walk—then that maple. . . . And I'll have them plant darling little flowers everywhere—" The new, manipulable flowers are like Bobik and Baby Sophie as compared to the hierarchical trees that oblige respect for past established values and cannot be manipulated as we please.

While the rest of the characters are frustrated in Act II (Vershinin gets no tea, Tuzenbach gets no candy, Kulygin gets no evening in congenial company, Rode gets no evening of dancing that he'd taken a nap to prepare for, the carnival people get no party), Natasha is the great opposite. She gets her troika ride with Protopopov.

Protopopov, from the first mention of him, is so dislikable Masha doesn't want him invited to the birthday dinner, even though he's sent a large cake. Irina had not even considered inviting him. As Natasha's masculine shadow, he stands for the same successful vulgarity of the town as she, but, aside from his laughable name, he does not have the funniness and particularity that make us accept Natasha as—however terrible—reality. Protopopov is just a statistical fact of existence.

In Act IV Natasha's desires are accomplished, or are about to be. Her husband minds the baby while Protopopov sits in the living room. All the Prozorov friends and members of the family leave or are driven out. Andrei, who has frequently remarked about her "noise," can be reprimanded for waking the baby with loud talk, Irina can be corrected about her belt, the trees can come down, and Natasha is *there*, a matriarchal Genghis Khan.

## RODE

PROPERTIES:   Noisy goodwill, gym class at the high school, companionship with Fedotik.

RODE AND FEDOTIK START OUT AS AN APPARENTLY INSEPARABLE BOBCHINSKY-DOBCHINSKY COUPLE, but instead of being identical twins they are fraternal and different.

Rode is innocently stupid, loud, and repetitive, but still a congenial member of the enclave group. The Prozorov family group somehow is not only a little bigger, but a little better, because of him. His absurdities, foibles are lovable rather than dislikable.

In an affecting end when he is tearfully embracing Tuzenbach several times and kissing Irina's hands twice, he has a tiny apotheosis when, with his one piece of imagination and unusualness in the play, he calls good-bye not only to people but to trees and, finally, with a child's wit, "Good-bye, echo."

## FEDOTIK

*Like wit and the comic, humour has in it a liberating element.
But it has also something fine and elevating which is lacking
in the other two ways of deriving pleasure from intellectual
activity. [This is] the ego's victorious assertion of its own
invulnerability. . . . It insists that it is impervious to wounds
dealt by the outside world, in fact, that these are merely
occasions for affording it pleasure.*
                                   *Sigmund Freud:* HUMOUR *(1928)*

PROPERTIES:   Gifts, guitar, hobbies, camera, solitaire.
HOW HE MAKES LIFE MEANINGFUL:   By giving gifts, having hobbies.

WITH THIS VERY SPECIALIZED EXISTENCE FEDOTIK is essentially generous, sweet, and happy. When he can't go to the carnival party, he responds only, "What a shame. I was counting on spending the evening, but if the little baby's sick . . . Tomorrow I'll bring him a toy." Even the farewell is expressed in terms of gifts and photography. The sorrow of parting from his friends is replaced by "official" annoyance of a photographer—"Do hold still." He adds enormously to the pleasant, sweet funniness of the play, giving a sense of niceness to the Prozorov group.

In his one appearance without Rode (during the fire) he adds extraordinary charm and life with his laughter and dancing when he says, "Burnt to ashes! Burnt to ashes. Everything I had in this world!" Again, the climactic Act III has caused or revealed a change. In Fedotik's case his hobbies seem to be merely a satisfactory substitute for something else—something serious, so that when he loses them and is stripped clean he responds joyously and beautifully with the superiority of a human being over circumstances.

## FERAPONT

*"Oh, Lord," he went on with anguish. "To have one peep at Moscow! To see mother Moscow if only in my dreams."*
                                        PEASANTS, *1897*

FERAPONT IS AN EASYGOING, NATURAL, FAIRLY FOOLISH OLD MAN. His incredibly distorted facts, parodying Chebutykin's newspaper facts, are, somehow, no less trivial and far more amusing. Both characters' non sequiturs flower and pebble and dapple the Vuillard household scenes.

Ferapont's deafness is a convenience for Andrei to say his soliloquies to, that tell the audience his private feelings and his public contacts with the county board and the Protopopov world. Ferapont's litmus-paper reactions to Andrei's moods are another convenience for revealing Andrei's changes, i.e., in Act II the good-humored Andrei calls him, "Ferapont, old man," while in Act III bad-tempered Andrei demands that Ferapont call him "your honor." This is further indicated—and at length—in the second half of the play when Ferapont seems more insistent and has a moment or two of superiority to Andrei when he, Ferapont, actually has to reason with him to get him to sign the papers.

The most important, strange, imaginative function of Ferapont is to parody Andrei's (and the sisters') Moscow dreams. His are the dreams of a big old dog who also dreams of magical Moscow. If his seem to discredit Moscow faintly, they also make it seem inevitable—that is, if doggy old Ferapont has them—that dreams *are* necessary, though his are more absurd than the others'.

Through Ferapont we see in Act IV Andrei's terrible fall in position when he, as a baby-wheeler, is replaced by Ferapont, the humbler one of the two humble servants. In the end, Ferapont and Andrei indistinguishably, absolutely similarly take care of the two children (one Andrei's, the other possibly Protopopov's) as commanded by Natasha.

Ferapont and Anfisa help give the feel of the Prozorov external family group, its servants, friends, and relatives. Both are pleasant, natural, mild and add to the pleasantness and humor of the play except when, through Natasha, they are treated badly.


### ANFISA

PROPERTIES:   The Prozorovs, Ferapont, later Olga, the government apartment.

ANFISA IS THE LITMUS PAPER from which we read indications about the three sisters, just as Ferapont is Andrei's litmus paper. In Act I, we see from Anfisa's behavior a continuation of the family group as it had been in former days. She treats Irina as a little girl, and in her mind the three sisters are the children they once were. In Act II this is extended and her position is so absolutely, immemorially established that, when she complains about Vershinin's leaving his tea and Masha gets angry at her, she not only is not afraid, but doesn't respond as a servant and, instead, makes an affectionate, good-humored response as though she is an important relative with a position that cannot be endangered. In

Act III, when she begs Olga not to drive her away, we are astonished and think how absurd. But then, when Natasha quarrels so violently in an attempt to get her thrown out, we realize that Anfisa is right (she's heard what Natasha surely has said before), and our knowledge of this is learned from her. In Act IV, in one of the most charming, happy, delightful changes in the play— something that partially counteracts the terrible changes—we see Anfisa at last entirely assured, happier than she's even been, singing a little aria of pure bliss about her humble happiness-situation in the government apartment with Olga.

\* \* \*

One ought to say about the whole minor group of Ferapont, Anfisa, Fedotik, and Rode, within the major group, that if these characters are removed, the play will be more terrible and unpleasant; a good deal of sweetness, charm, humor, and human inconsequentiality will disappear; and also, the feeling of the Prozorov extended family as a social group—the little enclave capable of fairly happy, good, continued existence unless destroyed —will disappear, too.

# IV / The Acts

Act i: *Beginnings*

TAKING PLACE AT NOON ON A SPRING DAY before the first leaves
come out, Act I is one of beginnings. Irina, the young girl whose
birthday it is, is beginning her new year quite recovered from
the death in the family and filled with happiness at the expectations
of going back to Moscow soon. We see Baron Tuzenbach's
beginning declarations of love for her. We see a friendship
beginning in the meeting of Colonel Vershinin and the social group
who, as Moscow speaking to Moscow, are immediately at ease
with each other and like each other at once. With Masha's "I'm
staying to lunch," we have the first intimation of her love affair
with Vershinin. While there is mention made that their brother
Andrei is beginning studies in Moscow to be a professor, he has
actually begun—by his proposal of marriage that day to Natasha,
"one of the local girls"—something quite different.

In this act occurs the establishment of a social situation that's
mostly very pleasant; mostly there are happy expectations,
mostly they are friendly and well-off. The Prozorovs and their
extensions—Anfisa and Ferapont, the family servants; Chebutykin,
the longtime family friend; Vershinin and the young officers
who knew the family or of it—*all* make a little, foreign, cultivated,
highly organized cell inside a provincial, crude city. The family is
a father-organization that has lost its father. General Prozorov
represented the days when they were governed, had their life
and ideals prescribed for them, and revolt, or breaking free for a
little space, was their only necessity. His censorship they obeyed,
or fooled. With it gone they can say anything; but in this
terrible freedom the vacancy of grown-ups who governed them
has to be filled by themselves, the new grown-ups. They had a

paradise in which they had only to follow the rules. Now they have to make the rules they follow—and they long to be in that earlier existence with Father. Moscow is their past, but just as definitely it is their future.

They are surviving partly happily, partly unhappily, in the midst of their uncultivated environment when the only son, who is the family's weakest element, introduces into it a powerful representative of the environment who manages to dominate him completely and, in the long run, to drive out the other members of the father-group. In the affectionate joking and teasing of part of the family by the rest are the first hints of anything troubling underneath the pleasant surface, and then we begin to see that Irina *is* partly troubled by life, that Masha is very much so, and that Olga is extreme and psychosomatic.

#### Act ii: *Continuations, Frustrations*

AFTER ACT I'S SPRING, NOON, Act II is between 8 and 9:30 at night in cold winter weather with the wind howling in the chimney. Act II begins with the continuation of the proposal: Here Natasha and Andrei are after a year or so of marriage, and the directness of their condition has a slap-in-the-face force. Here, also, is the continuation of Vershinin and Masha, of the "happiness" and "future" and meaning of life. The Andrei-Ferapont relationship is now fixed so that change can be indicated by change in it, i.e., Andrei's demanding to be called "your honor." There is a continuation of Tuzenbach's work-longing; with Irina there is the first dissatisfaction with her work. Act II is preparation for a party as is Act I, but a much more troubled preparation, which, when in full swing of beginning, is canceled out by Natasha (the provincial city element inside the little foreign cell, itself inside the provincial city), the element that's begun to destroy, grows and grows, and finally does destroy.

At the start of tea with singing, the little group is almost as pleasant as in the first act, but now needs the drunkenness, obliviousness, as in Act I it didn't. Being undermined by Natasha, the group continues more hectically with drinking and quarreling, and comes to nothing in a dreadfully anticlimactic, damped-out

way. Solyony's declaration of love to Irina is unpleasant nothing
to Irina, and results in unpleasant nothing to Solyony. The threat
about successful rivals brings out in the open the unpleasantness
toward Tuzenbach and Irina that finally kills Tuzenbach. Olga's
exhaustion leads her straight to bed. The exhausted Kulygin
doesn't get his evening in congenial company, and won't accompany
Vershinin who (still tealess) has had nothing to eat all day, has
to go out all alone. The act ends with most of them, and the
carnival people, frustrated in some way; all, except Natasha, who
gets her troika ride with Protopopov. Her temporary driving
away of most of the family in Act II is foreshadowing what will
happen permanently later. The stage is empty at the last with
Irina alone, saying yearningly, "To Moscow! To Moscow!
To Moscow!"

### ACT III: *Climaxes*

JUST AS THE TWO PRECEDING ACTS, this one is a large *social* thing
(Act I birthday dinner and Act II Mardi Gras preparations that
are canceled). Act III is carried along by the arrangements
necessitated by a social disaster, the fire in the town. The whole
household is either taking part or avoiding taking part in it. We
hardly notice what time of year it is. Under such unusual circumstances the unusual can be said or asked, and the extraordinary
truth about most of the characters comes out at this extraordinary
time.

   With all the climaxes in Act III: Olga and Natasha's quarrel,
Chebutykin's and Masha's confessions, Andrei's exposure, and
Irina's breaking down, the first announcement is made of the
brigade's leaving which will result in the departure of Vershinin
and the military attachments of the Prozorovs.

### ACT IV: *Conclusions*

THE SPRING AND BIRTH BEGINNINGS OF ACT I have proceeded to the
fall's prelude to winter, with the swans and geese flying south,
departures, death, and conclusions.

The enclave's allies are leaving, the last remnants of the father-organization are gone. Natasha has complete victory in the house. Irina and Olga have been driven out, and Masha no longer enters the house. Natasha has all the rooms she wants, she can chop the trees down, and she has Protopopov there every day. Natasha, by being introduced into the family-society of *The Three Sisters*, destroys it, just as Yelena's introduction into the family-society in *Uncle Vanya* disrupts it. But Yelena leaves, and that society reforms and tries to go on as before. Natasha has broken to pieces the Prozorov society whose fragments go on as best they can.

What to make of a diminished thing, how to get partial satisfaction, get along, make life on a lower level of expectation? They now regard this existence as necessary, their fate, their lot (like growing old) rather than as something escapable (like leaving for Moscow). Not living in Moscow is accepted.

Olga does this with her impersonal schoolwork and being head-mistress. No further mention of headaches and tiredness from her.

Irina plans to be satisfied without love, but with work away from home, and with marriage to a good man whom she doesn't love. This makes her feel happily anticipating again. When Tuzenbach is killed, the marriage part is removed, but she still sticks to the work ideal. Masha, after the partial satisfaction of the love affair with Vershinin, has to settle for continuing life without him but with Kulygin.

Chebutykin leaves for retirement, and Andrei surrenders in complete, abjectly nervous defeat.

In Act I Olga has the first lines and she recalled the band playing at the father's funeral. In Act IV Olga has the last lines to speak, and the band music accompanies her. As *The Three Sisters* ends, Olga puts her arms around the other two and makes a long speech that sums up her sisters' last words and one half of the play itself: the half that is about the meaning of life. She ends this speech by repeating the two Russian words that in an entirely literal translation would be *If knew, If knew*! and that in ordinary American English are *If only we knew, if only we knew*! Chebutykin once more sings his nonsensical little song and then says twice over the two Russian words that have ended three out of four of his last speeches, words which sum up the meaningless, senseless, hopeless half of life. "What's the difference?" Olga repeats, "If only we knew, if only we knew," and the play is over.

radiant
brow (6)
ecstasies (7)